FOUR POINT
Reading and Writing

1

INTERMEDIATE EAP

Series Editor: KEITH S. FOLSE

With contributions by
ROBYN BRINKS LOCKWOOD
KELLY SIPPELL
DOROTHY ZEMACH

Ann Arbor
University of Michigan Press

Copyright © by the University of Michigan 2011
All rights reserved
Published in the United States of America
The University of Michigan Press
Manufactured in the United States of America

∞ Printed on acid-free paper

ISBN-13: 978-0-472-03356-0

2014   2013   2012   2011   4   3   2   1

Acknowledgments

This book includes the contributions of three dedicated people: Robyn Brinks-Lockwood, Dorothy Zemach, and Kelly Sippell. Robyn and Kelly diligently and tirelessly kept the big picture of this series in mind as they completed the important task of locating readings on topics that would be appropriate for our academic-bound students as well as push our learners' English proficiency to the next level. Robyn and Kelly managed the difficult task of keeping the big picture of this book and the entire series in mind as they, with Dorothy, wrote the accompanying skills boxes and before, during, and after practice activities. Special thanks to Dorothy, who contributed many skills, activities, and other content to three of the six units. Special thanks also go to Robyn, whose work as developmental editor went above and beyond the call of normal duty. The quality of the material in this book is a testament to the hard work that all three of them invested here.

The publisher, series editor, and author would like to thank the educational professionals whose reviews helped shape the *Four Point* series and saw earlier versions of this material, particularly those from these institutions:

Auburn University
Boston University CELOP
Central Piedmont Community College
Colorado State University
Daytona Beach Community College
Duke University
Durham Technical College
Georgia State University
Harding University
Hillsborough Community College
Northern Virginia Community College, Alexandria Campus
Oregon State University
University of California, San Diego
University of Nevada at Las Vegas
University of North Carolina, Charlotte
Valencia Community College

Grateful acknowledgment is made to the following authors, publishers, and individuals for permission to reprint copyrighted or previously published materials.

Da Capo Publishers for *Structures or Why Things Don't Fall Down* by J.E. Gordon, © 1978.

HowStuffWorks.com for material on the Hubble Telescope in Unit 3 and on bridges in Unit 5.

MPTV Images for the photos on pages 115 and 132.

The National Aeronautics and Space Administration for the photo on page 97.

Prentice Hall for *Influence: Science and Practice, 5th ed.,* by Robert Cialdini, pp. 166–68, 199–203.

Random House for material: From *American Creation: Triumphs and Tragedies at the Founding of the Republic* by Joseph J. Ellis, copyright © 2007 by Joseph J. Ellis. Used by permission of Alfred A. Knopf, a division of Random House, Inc. From *Founding Brothers* by Joseph J. Ellis, copyright © 2000 by Joseph J. Ellis. Used by permission of Alfred A. Knopf, a division of Random House, Inc.

ThinkStock, Inc. for photos used in the book (except for the movie stills from "To Kill a Mockingbird.")

The University of Michigan Press for material in *Life, Death, and Entertainment in the Roman Empire,* edited by David Potter and D.J. Mattingly.

USA TODAY for "*To Kill a Mockingbird:* Endearing, Enduring at 50 Years" by Maria Puente. Used with permission.

Larry Zwier for writing text that appears in Units 2 and 3.

Every effort has been made to contact the copyright holders for permission to reprint borrowed material. We regret any oversights that may have occurred and will rectify them in future printings of this book.

Contents

4: Literature: *To Kill a Mockingbird*

Series Overview

Four Point is a four-volume series designed for English language learners (ELLs) whose primary goal is to succeed in an academic setting. While grammar points and learning strategies are certainly important, academic ELLs need skills-based books that focus on the four primary skills of reading, writing, listening, and speaking in a realistic, integrated format, as well as the two primary language bases of vocabulary and grammar. To this end, the ***Four Point*** series offers a unique combination of instructional material and activities that truly require students to read, write, listen, and speak in a multitude of combinations.

Four Point has two levels. Level 1 is designed for the first level of EAP instruction in a post-secondary institution. Level 2 follows for the subsequent level of EAP instruction. While academic listening and speaking skills are covered in one volume and academic reading and writing are covered in another, *all four skills are integrated throughout all books*, so a given task may focus on speaking and listening but have a reading and/or writing component to it as well.

Developing the Four Skills in *Four Point*

The series covers the four academic skills of reading, writing, listening and speaking while providing reinforcement and systematic recycling of key vocabulary and further exposure to grammar issues. The goal of this series is to help students improve their ability in each of these four critical skills and thereby enable the students to have sufficient English to succeed in their final academic setting, whether it be community college, college, or university.

Many ELLs report great difficulties upon entering their academic courses after they leave the safe haven of their English class with other nonnative speakers and their sympathetic and caring ESL teachers. Their academic instructors speak quickly, give long reading assignments due the next day, deliver classroom lectures and interactions at rapid, native speed, and sometimes balk at the excessive errors in their ELLs' writing. In sum, the ELL who has gone through a sheltered classroom setting is in for a rather rude awakening in a new learning situation where English is taken for granted and no one seems to understand the new reality of the dilemmas of ELLs. Through these materials, we hope to lessen the shock of such an awakening.

The activities in *Four Point* achieve the goal of helping our ELLs experience what life beyond the ESL classroom is like while they are still in our sheltered classroom. This chart explains some of the activities in *Four Point*:

Reading	Listening
Students will read longer, more difficult readings on interesting academic topics that represent the array of interests in a classroom. Students will get practice using strategies such as understanding difficult readings, SQ3R, and understanding the author's purpose.	Students will have to listen to both short conversations and academic discussions and long lectures to not only pick out details and facts but also practice picking up on speaker intentions or attitudes. Students will also gain experience listening to multiple native speakers at the same time.
Writing	**Speaking**
Students will write both short and long assignments. Special emphasis is given to the academic writing skills of paraphrasing and summarizing as well as understanding citations.	Students will practice both short and long extemporaneous speaking and thereby develop their speaking fluency, an area often overlooked in many ESL books. Students will also practice useful speaking phrases including persuading, expressing opinions, and agreeing and disagreeing.

Maximizing Coverage of the Two Primary Language Bases

ESL materials have come a long way from the old days of equating repetitive grammar drills for speaking practice or copying sentences for writing practice. However, in the ensuing shift from focus on language to focus on communication, very little was developed to address the needs of academic ELLs who need to do much more in English than engage in conversations about daily events, fill out job applications, or read short pieces of text for pleasure. It was the proverbial "baby being thrown out with the bath water" as emphasis on grammar and vocabulary was downplayed. However, in order to participate in academic settings, our ELLs certainly need focused activities to develop and then maintain their use of vocabulary and grammar. Toward this end, the *Four Point* series provides reinforcement of key grammar issues without overt practice activities.

More important, these books focus very heavily on vocabulary because ELLs realize that they are way behind their native-speaker counterparts when it comes to vocabulary. Each book highlights between 125–150 key vocabulary items, including individual words, compound words, phrasal verbs, short phrases, idioms, metaphors, collocations, and longer set lexical phrases. In learning vocabulary, the two most important features are frequency of retrievals (i.e., in exercises) and the spacing between these retrievals. Spaced rehearsal is accomplished in two ways. First, after words appear in a textbook, they will reappear multiple times afterward. Second, interactive web-based exercises provide more than ample opportunities for ELLs to practice their vocabulary learning through spaced rehearsals at (www.press.umich.edu/esl/compsite/4Point/).

General Overview of Units

Each of the books is divided into six units with numerous activities within each unit. The material in each of the volumes could be covered in ten to twelve weeks, but this number is flexible depending on the students and the teacher, and the depth to which the material is practiced.

Using the Exercises in This Book

Each unit includes two reading passages on the same topic within a field of academic study. The exercises accompanying the readings are meant to strengthen a range of reading and writing skills, notably:

- understanding the big picture
- developing vocabulary
- developing strategies for understanding academic texts through before reading, during reading, and after reading strategies
- paraphrasing
- summarizing
- synthesizing information

Special attention was given to providing material that would expose students to the types of texts and writing assignments that might be common in difficult academic disciplines. **The goal is to provide students with a variety of strategies/ tools to master whatever academic texts they may encounter. In addition, the inclusion of three types of reading strategies—before, during, and after—is unprecedented in ESL textbooks but is grounded in the realities of today's academic content and in the research on the strategies used by successful readers.**

Getting Started

The discussion questions before each reading passage should prompt students to begin thinking about relevant topics and issues. These discussions should be allowed to range freely.

Strategy/Skill Boxes

Other types of strategies and skills—primarily related to reading and writing—are highlighted at various points throughout the units. Each appears in a display box with a short explanation and is followed by an activity to explicitly practice what has been learned.

Reading for the Big Picture

Each reading in a unit is followed by short "big picture" questions. These questions are designed only to gauge student comprehension of the reading's main points after implementing the before, during, and after reading strategies.

Paraphrasing to Simplify

Every reading is accompanied by an exercise in producing focused paraphrases. These represent only the "core" of meaning in the originals. As in any paraphrase, the student has to recognize and produce alternate wording for the concepts in the original sentence. In a focused paraphrase, however, the student also has to distinguish the sentence's central proposition(s) from the "distractions" of extra modifiers, parenthetical asides, lists of examples, and so on. There are three production items, in which students compose their own focused paraphrases.

Short Writing Tasks: Summary and Research

Each unit has two prompts for writing short pieces related to the topic of the unit. Suggested lengths range from 5–7 sentences to 8–12 sentences. These are general guidelines only. Most of them could generate longer pieces of writing if the instructor wishes. The main aim at this point in the unit, however, is to push students' ability to include complex ideas in their writing.

Synthesizing: Writing Projects

Students are expected to proceed from what they learned via the reading passages to writing academically. Projects are designed to mimic actual assignments or test questions students are likely to encounter in their academic courses. One or two prompts are for pieces that could be written in a one-hour class period or part of a class period. Typically, these prompts encourage students to do some planning as homework before the in-class writing. There are two prompts per unit that require more outside reading and a longer finished product. They are meant to be assigned as homework assignments. The directions in such prompts ask students to do some light research. The suggested lengths are just that—suggestions.

These long writing assignments are not meant to be formal term papers. This book does not comprehensively address specific issues of formal academic citation, but it does discuss ways to acknowledge the sources of one's information (see Unit 1). Teachers are free, of course, to turn one or two of these writing projects into something longer, more formal, and with higher stakes. They are also free to skip these longer projects if time is short.

Emphasis on Vocabulary Learning

One of the best features of this book that separates it from other academic preparation books is the heavy focus on vocabulary. We recognize—as our students certainly do—that they face serious difficulties because of their limited vocabulary. The vocabulary levels of the best ELLs are often insufficient to cope with daily academic work, whether it be the vocabulary in a professor's lecture, the course book, a group discussion project, or a term paper. We would even go so far as to say that the single most important assistance we can give our students is to help them increase their academic vocabulary.

To meet this important lexical goal, our book explicitly teaches and practices a great deal of key vocabulary. First of all, the readings have not been watered down. In other words, they have not been rewritten in the traditional ESL-ese language. In addition, two or three unknown vocabulary items, especially those related to culture (e.g., the Great Depression), have been glossed within the text.

Each unit contains these activities: Vocabulary Power, Your Active Vocabulary, Rapid Vocabulary Review, and Vocabulary Log.

VOCABULARY POWER

Each unit contains two of these activities, each of which consists of eight vocabulary items in bold that students must match with the correct definitions. The vocabulary is used in context, so this activity practices vocabulary items in their natural context. This natural context is more difficult than the usual watered down material found in many ESL textbooks.

YOUR ACTIVE VOCABULARY IN THE REAL WORLD

In this activity, learners are given a list of ten vocabulary items from the readings. Learners are asked to decide whether a given word is more useful in their reading, writing, speaking, or listening. In this critical-thinking task, learners are expected to consider how they might actually need this new vocabulary item. We know vocabulary is important, but we cannot teach our learners all the words they need. Therefore, **a major goal of this book is to help train our learners to become active vocabulary seekers,** which means when they encounter a new word, they need to decide if the word is one they really need to know to be able to use in their writing or speaking or if they are more likely to hear that word in a lecture or conversation or read it in a passage. In other words, we want our learners to recognize the difference between words they need to be able to use and words they need to be able to recognize. These activities are designed to generate class discussion.

RAPID VOCABULARY REVIEW

This activity reviews all the target vocabulary in the unit. It is divided into two sections—synonyms and combinations and associations. The first is straightforward: One item out of three is closest in meaning to the target item, and students indicate which one it is. The second section involves more lateral thinking. The correct answer may stand in any of several relationships to the target term. It may complete a phrase involving the target item, it may name a category to which the target item belongs, or it may state an effect of which the target item is a cause. Some students may be unfamiliar with such a non-linear form of vocabulary review, but it is an essential part of comprehensive vocabulary study. Students should be encouraged to persevere.

VOCABULARY LOG

Crucial to the vocabulary acquisition process is the initial noticing of unknown vocabulary. ELLs must notice the vocabulary in some way, and this noticing then triggers awareness of the item and draws the learner's attention to the word in all subsequent encounters, whether the word is read in a passage or heard in a conversation or lecture. To facilitate noticing and then multiple retrievals of new vocabulary, we have included a chart listing approximately 20 to 25 key vocabulary items at the end of each unit. This Vocabulary Log has three columns and requires students to provide a definition or translation in the second column and then an original example or note about usage in the third column. As demonstrated in *Vocabulary Myths* (Folse 2004, University of Michigan Press), there is no research showing that a definition is better than a translation or vice-versa, so we suggest that you let ELLs decide which one they prefer. After all, this log is each student's individual vocabulary notebook, so students should use whatever information is helpful to the individual student and that will help the student remember and use the vocabulary item. If the log information is not deemed useful, the learner will not review this material—which defeats the whole purpose of keeping the notebook. In the third column, students can use the word in a phrase or sentence, or they can also add usage information about the word such as *usually negative, very formal sounding,* or *used only with the word* launch, for example.

1

Psychology: Human Behavior

Psychology is the study of the human mind. Psychologists investigate human behavior and feelings. The readings in this unit come from a particular branch of psychology that studies group behavior. The two principles examined here, the association principle and the scarcity principle, explain some aspects of why people in crowds or groups behave the way they do.

Part 1: The Association Principle

Getting Started

Sports fans are known for their strong loyalty to teams who come from their country (when playing internationally) or who come from their hometown or the university that they attended (when playing nationally). This is true even if the fans have never played the game and do not know the athletes personally. Answer these questions with a partner.

1. What sports teams are associated with your hometown or university? Have you ever watched their games live, on TV, or online?

   _____

   _____

   _____

   _____

2. Do you consider yourself a loyal fan to any of these teams? Why or why not?

   _____

   _____

   _____

   _____

3. What do you think are some reasons that fans support local teams?

   _____

   _____

   _____

   _____

Reading 1 is from a popular psychology textbook titled *Influence: Science and Practice*. This excerpt discusses how the association principle explains the attachment sports fans have to their teams. The association principle holds that if you connect two things—for example, a celebrity and the brand of soft drink he or she is advertising—you will transfer the opinions you have about the first thing (you think the celebrity is popular and fashionable) to the second (therefore, the soft drink must be popular and fashionable too).

Before reading an academic passage, it is useful to skim the text by quickly checking for key features and information.

Before Reading Strategy: Skimming

Skimming is a pre-reading strategy that will help you read more quickly and with greater understanding. **Skimming is not reading.** You are only looking quickly at some key information.

1. First, check the title of the article or chapter. Notice the length of the passage. This will give you an idea of how long it will take you to read it.

2. Then read the introduction, the first one or two sentences in each paragraph, and the conclusion.

3. Notice if there are features such as illustrations, graphs and charts, or bold or italic words that indicate key vocabulary.

4. Read any questions or exercises connected with the reading.

By doing these four things, you will have an idea of the main points in the reading. Skimming will make it easier for you to both understand and remember important information as you read it.

Practice Activity: Skimming

Skim Reading 1, and answer the questions. Do <u>not</u> read slowly and carefully. See how quickly you can find the answers. Raise your hand as soon as you are finished to show your instructor that you have finished.

1. The reading is _____ pages long.

   a. two

   b. three

   c. four

2. Paragraph 2 is mostly _____.

   a. a story that gives an example of how serious sports fans are

   b. an explanation of why sports fans feel strongly

   c. a connection between the association principle and medical care

3. The reading is mostly about _____.

   a. how sports is like business

   b. problems caused by sports fans

   c. the behavior of sports fans

During Reading Strategy: Annotating as You Read

Annotating means summarizing the most important information in each paragraph as you read. You cannot summarize without understanding what you've read, so it is a useful way to check comprehension. In addition, you are creating a useful study guide that you can use to participate during class discussions and to study for tests. You can write your notes in the margin or on sticky notes.

When you annotate, you can also circle or underline main ideas and definitions. You might wish to note the purpose of some paragraphs; for example, a story used to explain a point you could mark as "example." Look at this example of how the first paragraph of Reading 1 could be annotated:

A lot of strange behavior can be explained by the fact that people understand the (association principle) well enough to try to <u>link themselves to positive events</u> and <u>separate themselves from negative events</u>—even when they have not caused the events. Some of the strangest of such behavior takes place in the great arena of sports. The actions of athletes are not the issue, though. After all, in the heated contact of the game, they are entitled to an occasional eccentric outburst. Instead, it is the often raging, irrational, boundless fervor of <u>sports fans</u> that seems, on its face, so puzzling. How can we account for wild sports riots in Europe, or the murder of players and referees by South American soccer crowds gone berserk,* or the unnecessary lavishness of gifts provided by local fans to already wealthy American ballplayers on the special "day" set aside to honor them? Rationally, none of this makes sense. It's just a game! Isn't it?	*intro:* *the association principle—people want to be connected to pos. events and not to neg. events* *sports fans = very passionate about their team* *berserk = crazy* *WHY?*

Practice Activity: Annotating

Read the sentences from another source about sports fans, and re-state the main idea in your own words. Compare your annotations with a partner.

1. A recent survey shows that teenage boys are the most enthusiastic sports fans, possibly because of their own involvement in playing sports. However, they are less likely than older males to watch live sports matches on television. Instead, they rely on summaries of the games on televised news programs or the Internet.	
2. Women between the ages of 25 and 34 are the least interested in sports. Teenage girls are major sports fans, though they don't watch a lot of sports on television. After age 35, women show more interest in watching televised sports, especially with friends and family.	
3. When men over the age of 50 watch sports, it's usually with a female friend or family member. While younger men, especially in the 25–34 age range, turn to the Internet for sports coverage, men over the age of 50 are far less likely to, though they may spend more time listening to sports on the radio.	

Vocabulary Power

There are a number of terms and phrases in this reading that you may encounter in other academic settings. Add at least five vocabulary items to your vocabulary notebook or log.

Match the words in bold from the reading on the left with a definition on the right.

1. _____ It is serious, intense, and **highly** personal.

2. _____ There are two important lessons to be **derived** from this true story.

3. _____ When viewed in this **light**, the passion of a sports fan begins to make sense.

4. _____ Perhaps the twin desires to connect ourselves to winners and to distance ourselves from losers were combined perfectly in the **remarks** of one particular student.

5. _____ A lot of strange behavior can be explained by the fact that people understand the association principle well enough to try to **link** themselves to positive events and separate themselves from negative events—even when they have not caused the events.

6. _____ Have you noticed for example, how often after a home-team victory fans crowd into the view of a TV camera, **thrust** their index fingers high, and shout, "We're number one! We're number one!"

7. _____ Some of the students were asked the **outcome** of a certain game their team lost; the other students were asked the **outcome** of a different game—one their team had won.

8. _____ The second lesson reveals much about the nature of the union of sports and sports fans, something **crucial** to its basic character: It is a personal thing.

a. taken, concluded, learned

b. connect

c. result

d. very

e. important, essential

f. comments, words

g. manner, way

h. push with force

Reading

Now, read the passage. Check your comprehension by annotating in the margins as you read.

The Passion of Sports Fans

(1) A lot of strange behavior can be explained by the fact that people understand the association principle well enough to try to link themselves to positive events and separate themselves from negative events—even when they have not caused the events. Some of the strangest of such behavior takes place in the great arena of sports. The actions of athletes are not the issue, though. After all, in the heated contact of the game, they are entitled to an occasional eccentric outburst. Instead, it is the often raging, irrational, boundless fervor of sports fans that seems, on its face, so puzzling. How can we account for wild sports riots in Europe, or the murder of players and referees by South American soccer crowds gone berserk,* or the unnecessary lavishness of gifts provided by local fans to already wealthy American ballplayers on the special "day" set aside to honor them? Rationally, none of this makes sense. It's just a game! Isn't it?

berserk:
energetically violent

(2) Hardly. The relationship between sport and an earnest fan is anything but game-like. It is serious, intense, and highly personal. A good illustration comes from an anecdote: It concerns a World War II soldier who returned to his home in the Balkans after the war and shortly thereafter stopped speaking. Medical examinations could find no physical cause for the problem. There was no wound, no brain damage, no vocal impairment. He could read, write, understand a conversation, and follow orders. Yet he would not talk—not for his doctors, not for his friends, not even for his family. Perplexed and exasperated, his doctors moved him to another city and placed him in a veteran's hospital where he remained for 30 years, never breaking his self-imposed silence and sinking into a life of social isolation. Then one day, a radio in his ward* happened to be tuned to a soccer match between his hometown team and a traditional rival. When at a crucial point of play the referee called a foul against a player from the mute* veteran's home team, he jumped from his chair, glared at the radio, and spoke his first words in more than three decades: "You dumb ass!"* he cried. "Are you trying to *give* them the match?" With that, he returned to his chair and to a silence he never again broke.

> **ward:** section of a hospital
>
> **mute:** unable or unwilling to speak; silent
>
> **dumb ass:** (very informal, slang) a stupid, unintelligent, or unskilled person

(3) There are two important lessons to be derived from this true story. The first concerns the sheer power of the phenomenon. The veteran's desire to have his hometown team succeed was so strong that it alone produced a deviation from his firmly established way of life. The second lesson reveals much about the nature of the union of sports and sports fans, something crucial to its basic character: It is a personal thing. Whatever fragment of an identity that damaged, mute man still possessed was engaged by soccer play. No matter how weakened his ego may have become after 30 years of silence in a hospital ward, it was involved in the outcome of the match. Because he, personally, would be diminished by a hometown defeat, and he, personally, would be enhanced by a hometown victory. How? Through the principle of association. The mere connection of birthplace hooked him, wrapped him, tied him to the approaching triumph or failure.

(4) As distinguished author Isaac Asimov (1975) put it describing our reactions to the contests we view, "All things being equal, you root for your own sex, your own culture, your own locality . . . and what you want to prove is that *you* are better than the other person. Whomever you root for represents *you*; and when he [or she] wins, *you* win." When viewed in this light, the passion of a sports fan begins to make sense. The game is no light diversion to be enjoyed for its inherent form* and artistry. **inherent form:** built-in, already existing structure The self is at stake. That is why hometown crowds are so adoring and, more tellingly, so grateful toward those regularly responsible for home-team victories. That is also why the same crowds are often ferocious in their treatment of players, coaches, and officials they feel are responsible for athletic failures.

(5) So we want our affiliated sports teams to win to prove our own superiority, but to whom are we trying to prove it? Ourselves, certainly, but to everyone else, too. According to the association principle, if we can surround ourselves with success that we are connected with in even a superficial way (for example, place of residence), our public prestige will rise.

(6) All this says is that we purposefully manipulate the visibility of our connections with winners and losers in order to make ourselves look good to anyone who views these connections. By showcasing the positive associations and burying the negative ones, we are trying to get observers to think more highly of us and to like us more. There are many ways we go about this, but one of the simplest and most pervasive is in the pronouns we use. Have you noticed, for example, how often after a home-team victory fans crowd into the range of a TV camera, thrust their index fingers high, and shout, "We're number one! We're number one!" Note that the call is not, "They're number one" or even "Our team is number one." The pronoun is *we*, designed to imply the closest possible identity with the team.

(7) Note also that nothing similar occurs in the case of failure. No television viewer will ever hear the chant, "We're in last place! We're in last place!" Hometeam defeats are the times for distancing oneself. Here *we* is not nearly as preferred as the insulating pronoun *they*. To prove the point, I once did a small experiment in which students at Arizona State University were phoned and asked to describe the outcome of a football game their school had played a few weeks earlier (Cialdini et al., 1976). Some of the

students were asked the outcome of a certain game their team lost; the other students
were asked the outcome of a different game—one their team had won. My fellow
researcher, Avril Thorne, and I simply listened to what was said and recorded the
percentage of students who used the word *we* in their descriptions. When the results
were tabulated, it was obvious that the students had tried to connect themselves to
success by using the pronoun *we* to describe their school-team victory—"We beat
Houston, 17 to 14" or "We won." In the case of the lost game, however, *we* was rarely
used. Instead, the students used terms designed to keep themselves separate from their
defeated team—"They lost to Missouri, 30 to 20," or "I don't know the score, but Arizona
State got beat." Perhaps the twin desires to connect ourselves to winners and to
distance ourselves from losers were combined perfectly in the remarks of one particular
student. After dryly recounting the score of the home-team defeat—"Arizona State lost
it, 30 to 20"—he blurted in anguish, "*They* threw away *our* chance for a national
championship!"

   (8) The tendency to trumpet one's links to victors is not unique to the sports arena.
After general elections in Belgium, researchers looked to see how long it took
homeowners to remove their lawn-signs favoring one or another political party.
According to Boen et al. (2002)[†], the better the election result for a party, the
longer homeowners wallowed in* the positive connection by leaving the
signs up.

> **wallowed in:**
> spent a lot of time
> enjoying, often to
> an extreme degree

[†]In-text citations are explained on page 28.

After Reading Strategy: Summarizing

Summarizing means identifying the main points of the reading and stating them in your own words. If you can summarize a reading, you know you have understood it.

How detailed your summary is will depend on your purpose for reading. For example, if you are reading for background information, a basic summary will be enough. If you need to understand the reading's main ideas as well as be able to explain examples to prepare for a discussion or a test, your summary should be more detailed. In either case, a summary is much shorter than the original.

Your annotations will be very useful in writing your summary, since they should already express the main ideas in your own words.

Practice Activity: Summarizing

Work with the same partner for each task.

1. Take turns. Re-read your annotation for one paragraph, and then cover it. Re-state the points in your own words. Your partner will compare your version with his or her version.

2. Take turns. Explain the purpose of each paragraph. Use phrases such as *It explains the important concept of . . . , It gives an example of . . . , It explains why. . . .*

3. Think about the information in each paragraph. Which paragraphs show essential information? Which paragraphs do not?

Practice Activity: Reading for the Big Picture

Choose the best answer to each question.

1. What is the main idea of the passage?

    a. Sports fans have stronger feelings than people who are not sports fans. That is why they can be more likely to commit violent behavior or to have unusual reactions.

    b. Sports fans' loyalty to their teams is not rational. It cannot be understood through logic.

    c. Sports fans support their teams because they feel a personal connection through a shared common origin.

    d. Sports fans support teams when they win, but they don't pay as much attention to or may even dislike teams that lose.

2. Which best describes the association principle as it relates to sports?

    a. Sports fans link themselves to their sports teams whether they win or lose.

    b. Sports fans have a serious and rational relationship with their teams.

    c. Sports fans often cause the events they later separate themselves from.

    d. Sports fans like being associated with a good sports team, even if it is only superficial.

Paraphrasing to Simplify

Write a paraphrase that expresses the main points of the original without re-using too many words or phrases from the original.

1. The veteran's desire for his hometown team to succeed was so strong that it alone produced a deviation from his established way of life.

   _____

   _____

   _____

2. By showcasing the positive associations and burying the negative ones, we are trying to get observers to think more highly of us and to like us more.

   _____

   _____

   _____

3. According to the association principle, if we can surround ourselves with success that we are connected with even in a superficial way (for example, place of residence), our public prestige will rise.

   _____

   _____

   _____

Writing Strategy: Writing a Summary

A summary explains the main ideas and most important supporting ideas of a reading in your own words. A summary should give the title, author, and source of the reading.

Look at these common ways to introduce or note the source for summaries:

> In her article *Women Sports Fans: A Different Purpose?* from the online website <u>Sportsfans.com</u> (April 11, 2010), researcher Ellen Dover explains that. . . .

> Women watch sports for different reasons than men (Ellen Dover, *Women Sports Fans: A Different Purpose?* <u>Sportsfans.com</u>, April 11, 2010).

> According to Ellen Dover, a behavioral scientist and researcher, men and women watch sports for different reasons. Her article *Women Sports Fans: A Different Purpose?* (<u>Sportsfans.com</u>, April 11, 2010) explains three main differences.

Besides using your own words to summarize the main ideas, there are a few other tips to follow.

- Do not include details (a summary is shorter than the original).

- Do not include your own opinions or ideas.

- Do not change the author's original idea or meaning or to include incorrect statements while you paraphrase.

- Use your own words and sentence structure.

Practice Activity: Writing a Summary

Write a summary of this passage from a book about traveling to Australia by Bill Bryson. Include the main ideas and only the most important supporting details. Be sure to list the source. Refer to the box on page 15 to review the strategy and tips.

Each time you fly from North America to Australia, and without anyone asking how you feel about it, a day is taken away from you when you cross the international date line. I left Los Angeles on January 3 and arrived in Sydney fourteen hours later on January 5. For me there was no January 4. None at all. Where it went exactly I couldn't tell you. All I know is that for one twenty-four-hour period in the history of earth, it appears I had no being.

I find that a little uncanny, to say the least. I mean to say, if you were browsing through your ticket folder and you saw a notice that said, "Passengers are advised that on some crossings twenty-four-hour loss of existence may occur" (which is, of course, how they would phrase it, as if it happened from time to time), you would probably get up and make inquiries, grab a sleeve, and say, "Excuse me." There is, it must be said, a certain metaphysical comfort in knowing that you can cease to have material form and it doesn't hurt at all, and, to be fair, they do give you the day back on the return journey when you cross the date line in the opposite direction and thereby manage to somehow arrive in Los Angeles *before* you left Sydney, which in its way, of course, is an even neater trick.

Now, I vaguely understand the principles involved here. I can see that there has to be a notional line where one day ends and the next begins, and that when you cross that line temporal oddities will necessarily follow. But that still doesn't get away from the fact that on any trip between America and Australia you will experience something that would be, in any other circumstance, the starkest impossibility. However hard you train

or concentrate or watch your diet, no matter how many steps you take on the

StairMaster, you are never going to get so fit that you can cease to occupy space for

twenty-four hours or be able to arrive in one room before you left the last one.

So there is a certain sense of achievement just in arriving in Australia—a pleasure

and satisfaction to be able to step from the airport terminal into dazzling antipodean

sunshine and realize that all your many atoms, so recently missing and unaccounted for,

have been reassembled in an approximately normal manner (less half a pound or so of

brain cells that were lost while watching a Bruce Willis movie). In the circumstances, it

is a pleasure to find yourself anywhere; that it is Australia is a positive bonus.

From *In a Sunburned Country*, by Bill Bryson, New York: Broadway Books, 2001.

Short Writing Tasks

Write your response to each task following the directions given for length and source material.

Task 1 (Summary)

> Look again at Reading 1. Write a one-paragraph summary of the reading. Do not simply copy from the reading. A suggested approach is to make a list of key words and main ideas from the reading and then to not look at the reading again. Review the box on page 15. Use only your notes as you prepare your own summary. Be sure to mention or cite your source. (Length: 5–7 sentences)

_____

_____

_____

_____

_____

_____

_____

Task 2 (Research)

> Reading 1 talks about wild sports fans. Based on your instructor's guidelines, do some light research online or in a library to find an example of a sporting event and its fans. Light research is not as detailed and does not take as much time as preparation for a long essay or research paper. Light research includes finding a few sources that provide some supporting details. Write about the event and describe who played, the event's importance, the role of the fans, and the results of the event. Take notes in the space provided. Then write your paragraph on a separate piece of paper. (Length: 5–7 sentences)

_____

_____

_____

_____

_____

_____

Part 2: The Scarcity Principle

Getting Started

The word *scarcity* refers to how rare or unusual something is. In general, items are more valuable when they are less common; gold costs more than iron not because it is more attractive or more useful, but because there is less of it. This principle also explains why people want something that they cannot have: they assume it is more valuable because it is not available. Answer these questions with a partner.

1. Think of three materials or products that are rare. Are they also expensive? Can you think of any rare items that are not expensive?

   _____

   _____

   _____

   _____

2. What other factors can cause a material or product to be valuable or expensive (for example, usefulness)? What factors can cause a material or product to be unimportant or inexpensive?

   _____

   _____

   _____

   _____

3. Think of one expensive thing that you own and one cheap thing that you own. What are the factors that make the first one expensive and the second one cheap?

   _____

   _____

   _____

   _____

Reading 2 is also from the popular psychology textbook *Influence: Science and Practice*. It discusses how an understanding of the scarcity principle can be used to influence behavior, whether to get students or patients to take certain actions or to get customers to buy more products.

You will read more quickly and understand academic passages better if you activate background knowledge about the topic before you read.

Before Reading Strategy: Activating Background Knowledge

You probably have some knowledge, however small, about almost every topic that you read about. Activating this background knowledge will help you learn new information more effectively and comprehend what you read more easily. To *activate* something means to set it in motion; think of charging a battery, for example, or flipping the switch that turns on a machine.

1. Make sure you know the topic of the reading before you begin. Check the title and any introductory information. Skim the reading.

2. Take a few minutes to think about what you already know about the topic. It is useful to talk with a classmate, both to put your ideas into words and to hear your classmate's information; however, even thinking silently to yourself is useful. Consider information you have heard or read before, general impressions about the topic, and questions you have.

3. Think about what vocabulary will be used to discuss the topic. What words and phrases do you already know and associate with that topic? Is there any vocabulary you know in another language but not in English? Consider looking words up in advance. You might meet that vocabulary in the reading, or you might just use it later for discussions or writing assignments.

Practice Activity: Activating Background Knowledge

Work with a partner. For each topic listed, take notes on a separate piece of paper about (1) what you already know about the topic and (2) what words and phrases you think would appear in a reading about that topic. Spend no more than ten minutes on each topic (five minutes for each set of notes).

Note: The first two topics are related to the general subject of Reading 2 but are not directly addressed. The final topic is the one covered in the reading. Keep your notes from #3 to check after you have finished the reading.

1. reasons that stores put items on sale

2. the effects of over-praising children (giving them too many compliments too often)

3. how the scarcity principle affects the value of an item and how badly a customer wants it

During Reading Strategy: Keeping a Vocabulary Log

During academic reading, you will encounter a lot of vocabulary. Most words you will already know, but some will be new. Many vocabulary words will be words that you will see again in other academic readings and in other disciplines. Therefore, it is important to notice those as you read and keep a vocabulary log.

Keeping a log is a good strategy to use to increase your vocabulary. You will have your words in a notebook and can easily retrieve the definition or notes later. There are many ways to keep a vocabulary log, but it is a good idea to include columns for the vocabulary word or phrase, its definition or translation, and your use of it in a short phrase or sentence or your note that helps you remember it.

A vocabulary log is included in every unit of this textbook (see pages 35–36 for an example), but you may also want to keep a separate notebook reserved for only vocabulary. A sample vocabulary log might look like this:

Vocabulary Item	Definition or Translation	Your Original Phrase, Sentence, or Note
an item	one thing	I bought 3 items.

Practice Activity: Building a Vocabulary Log

Read these sentences from Reading 1, and fill in your vocabulary log with the given underlined words.

1. A lot of strange behavior can be explained by the fact that people understand the association principle well enough to try to <u>link</u> themselves to positive events and separate themselves from negative events—even when they have not caused the events.

2. How can we account for . . . the unnecessary <u>lavishness</u> of gifts provided by local fans to already wealthy American ballplayers on the special "day" set aside to honor them?

3. Because he, personally, would be diminished by a hometown defeat, and he, personally, would be <u>enhanced</u> by a hometown victory.

4. The mere connection of birthplace <u>hooked</u> him, wrapped him, tied him to the approaching <u>triumph</u> or failure.

5. That is also why the same crowds are often <u>ferocious</u> in their treatment of players, coaches, and officials <u>implicated</u> in athletic failures.

Vocabulary Item	Definition or Translation	Your Original Phrase, Sentence, or Note
link		

Vocabulary Power

There are a number of terms and phrases in this reading that you may encounter in other academic settings. Add at least five vocabulary items to your vocabulary notebook or log.

Match the words in bold from the reading on the left with a definition on the right.

1. _____ Collectors of everything from baseball cards to antiques are keenly aware of the scarcity principle's influence in determining the **worth** of an item.

2. _____ Take as evidence the experience of Florida State University students who, like most undergraduates when **surveyed**, rated the quality of their campus cafeteria food unsatisfactory.

3. _____ Especially under conditions of **risk** and uncertainty, the threat of potential loss plays a powerful role in human decision making.

4. _____ Health researchers Alexander Rothman and Peter Salovey have applied this **insight** into the medical arena, where individuals are frequently urged to undergo tests to detect existing illnesses. . . .

5. _____ People seem to be more **motivated** by the thought of losing something than by the thought of gaining something of equal value.

6. _____ There are all sorts of cues that **tip off** such interest—closer-than-normal examination of the appliance, a casual look at any instruction booklets associated with the appliance, discussions held in front of the appliance, but no attempt to seek out a salesperson for further information.

7. _____ Probably the most **straightforward** use of the scarcity principle occurs in the "limited-number" tactic in which a customer is informed that a certain product is in short supply that cannot be guaranteed to last long.

8. _____ In each instance, however, the **intent** was to convince customers of an item's scarcity and thereby increase its immediate value in their eyes.

a. danger

b. value

c. pushed, influenced

d. understanding, ideas, thoughts

e. indicate, show, reveal

f. direct, obvious

g. asked

h. purpose

Reading

Now, read the passage. Mark words to add to your vocabulary log as you read.

Less Is Best and Loss Is Worst

(1) Almost everyone is vulnerable to the scarcity principle in some form. Take as evidence the experience of Florida State University students who, like most undergraduates when surveyed, rated the quality of their campus cafeteria food unsatisfactory. Nine days later, according to a second survey, they had changed their

minds. Something had happened to make them like their cafeteria's food significantly better than before. Interestingly, the event that caused them to shift their opinions had nothing to do with the quality of the food service, which had not changed a whit.* But its availability had. On the day of the second survey, the students learned that, because of a fire, they could not eat at the cafeteria for the next two weeks (West, 1975).

whit: the smallest part of something (to not change a whit: to not change at all)

(2) Collectors of everything from baseball cards to antiques are keenly aware of the scarcity principle's influence in determining the worth of an item. As a rule, if an item is rare or becoming rare, it is more valuable. Especially enlightening on the importance of scarcity in the collectible market is the phenomenon of the "precious mistake." Flawed items—a blurry stamp or double-struck* coin—are sometimes the most valued of all. Thus, a stamp carrying a three-eyed likeness of George Washington is anatomically incorrect, aesthetically unappealing, and yet highly sought after.* There is instructive irony here: Imperfections that would otherwise make for rubbish* make for prized possessions when they bring along a lasting scarcity.

double-struck: on a metal coin, a defect caused by a machine stamping an image twice instead of once, resulting in two imprints in slightly different places

sought after: looked for; wanted or desired

make for rubbish: be trash

(3) Since my own encounter with the scarcity principle—*that opportunities seem more valuable to us when they are less available*—I have begun to notice its influence over a whole range of my actions. For instance, I routinely will interrupt an interesting face-to-face conversation to answer the ring of an unknown caller. In such a situation, the caller possesses a compelling feature that my face-to-face partner does not—potential unavailability. If I don't take that call, I might miss it (and the information it carries) for good. Never mind that the present conversation may be highly engaging or important—much more than I could reasonably expect an average phone call to be. With each unanswered ring, the phone interaction becomes less retrievable. For that reason and for that moment, I want it more than the other conversation.

(4) People seem to be more motivated by the thought of losing something than by the thought of gaining something of equal value (Hobfoll, 2001). For instance, college students experienced much stronger emotions when asked to imagine losses as opposed to gains in their romantic relationships or in their grade point averages (Ketelaar, 1995). Especially under conditions of risk and uncertainty, the threat of potential loss plays a powerful role in human decision making (Tversky & Kahneman, 1981; De Dreu & McCusker, 1997). Health researchers Alexander Rothman and Peter Salovey have applied this insight to the medical arena, where individuals are frequently urged to undergo tests to detect existing illnesses (e.g., mammography procedures, HIV screenings, cancer self-examinations). Because such tests involve the risk that a disease will be found and the uncertainty will be cured, messages stressing potential losses are most effective (Rothman & Salovey, 1997; Rothman, Martino, Bedell, Detweiler, & Salovey, 1999). For example, pamphlets advising young women to check for breast cancer through self-examinations are significantly more successful if they state their case in terms of what stands to be lost rather than gained (Meyerwitz & Chaiken, 1987). In the world of business, research has found that managers weigh potential losses more heavily than potential gains (Shelley, 1994). Even our brains seem to have evolved to protect us against loss in that it is more difficult to disrupt good decision-making regarding loss than gain (Weller et al., 2007).

Limited Numbers

(5) With the scarcity principle operating so powerfully on the worth we assign things, it is natural that sales and marketing professionals will do some similar operating of their own. Probably the most straightforward use of the scarcity principle occurs in the "limited-number" tactic in which a customer is informed that a certain product is in short supply that cannot be guaranteed to last long. During the time I was researching compliance strategies by infiltrating various organizations, I saw the limited-number tactic employed repeatedly in a range of situations: "There aren't more than five convertibles with this engine left in the state. And when they're gone, that's it, 'cause we're not making 'em anymore." "This is one of only two unsold corner lots* in the entire development. You wouldn't want the other one; it's got a nasty east-west exposure." "You may want to think seriously about buying more than one case today because production is backed way up and there's no telling when we'll get any more in."

corner lots: land that sits where two streets meet

(6) Sometimes the limited-number information was true, sometimes it was wholly false. In each instance, however, the intent was to convince customers of an item's scarcity and thereby increase its immediate value in their eyes. I admit to developing a grudging admiration for the practitioners who made this simple device work in a multitude of ways and styles. I was most impressed, however, with a particular version that extended the basic approach to its logical extreme by selling a piece of merchandise at its scarcest point—when it seemingly could no longer be had. The tactic was played to perfection in one appliance store I investigated where 30 to 50 percent of the stock was regularly

listed on sale. Suppose a couple in the store seemed, from a distance, to be moderately interested in a certain sale item. There are all sorts of cues that tip off such interest—closer-than-normal examination of the appliance, a casual look at any instruction booklets associated with the appliance, discussions held in front of the appliance, but no attempt to seek out a salesperson for further information. After observing the couple so engaged, a salesperson might approach and say, "I see you're interested in this model here, and I can understand why: it's a great machine at a great price. But, unfortunately, I sold it to another couple not more than 20 minutes ago. And, if I'm not mistaken, it was the last one we had."

(7) The customers' disappointment registers unmistakably. Because of its lost availability, the appliance suddenly becomes more attractive. Typically, one of the customers asks if there is any chance that an unsold model still exists in the store's back room or warehouse or other location. "Well," the salesperson allows, "that is possible, and I'd be willing to check. But do I understand that this is the model you want and if I can get it for you at this price, you'll take it?" Therein lies the beauty of the technique. In accord with the scarcity principle, the customers are asked to commit to buying the appliance when it looks least available and therefore most desirable. Many customers do agree to purchase at this singularly vulnerable time. Thus, when the salesperson (invariably) returns with the news than an additional supply of the appliance has been found, it is also with a pen and sales contract in hand. The information that the desired model is in good supply actually may make some customers find it less attractive again (Schwarz, 1984), although by then the business transaction has progressed too far for most people to renege.* The purchase decision made and committed to publicly at an earlier crucial point still holds. They buy.

> **renege:** to go back on; to fail to fulfill a promise or agreement

After Reading Strategy: Understanding Citations and Bibliographic Entries

Many academic works use information from other experts or publications. When this happens, the author needs to let the reader know the material came from another source.

As a reader, you need to recognize when the author is giving credit to another source. In-text citations are easy to recognize. Although there are several formats, a common method is to include the original author's last name and the year of the original work in parentheses at the end of borrowed material.

> In the world of business, research has found that managers weigh potential losses more heavily than potential gains (Shelley, 1994).

If you need more information about the original sources, you can then search for the bibliographic entry on the paper's Works Cited page or in its Bibliography, where the sources are arranged in alphabetical order by the original author's last name. For this example, you would search for Shelley because that is the author's last name. The bibliographic entry will include complete information for the source so that you can find Shelley's article, book, or website. The bibliographic entry for Shelley in 1994 would look like this:

> Shelley, M.K. (1994). Individual differences in lottery evaluation models. *Organizational Behavior and Human Decision Processes*, 73, 206–230.

This entry includes the author's name, publication date, the title of the article, the title of the journal or book where the text appeared, the volume number, and the page numbers. If it's an online article, the name of the website and the web address are usually included. This entry is in APA style. You need to check with your instructors and your department so that you use the format and punctuation that is desirable.

Note that the phrase *et al.* appears in in-text citations when there are more than three authors of the text. See pages 11 and 25 for examples.

Understanding citations and bibliographic entries will help you do more research when you need to write your own paper or read other sources on the same topic.

Practice Activity: Understanding Bibliographic Entries

Read the bibliographic entry for Reading 2. Identify the pieces of information.

Cialdini, R.B. (2009). *Influence: Science and Practice,* 5th ed. New York: Allyn and Bacon.

1. Author: _____

2. Title: _____

3. Publication Year: _____

4. Publisher: _____

Practice Activity: Reading for the Big Picture

Circle the correct information about the reading.

1. Collectors of items such as stamps and coins *are / are not* aware of the effects of the scarcity principle.

2. The best motivation for checking for breast cancer is *the attraction of improving future appearance or health / the fear of losing a breast or life to cancer.*

3. Business managers are more motivated by *making more money / not losing money they already have.*

4. When salespeople use the limited-number tactic, they are *always / sometimes* telling the truth.

5. If a customer finds out that an item she thought was unavailable actually is still available, she might buy it even though it seems less attractive now *if she already told the salesperson she would / because she thinks it will become unavailable again.*

Paraphrasing to Simplify

Write a paraphrase that expresses the main points of the original without re-using too many words or phrases from the original.

1. With the scarcity principle operating so powerfully on the worth we assign things, it is natural that sales and marketing professionals will do some similar operating of their own.

   _____

   _____

   _____

   _____

2. Probably the most straightforward use of the scarcity principle occurs in the "limited-number" tactic in which a customer is informed that a certain product is in short supply that cannot be guaranteed to last long.

   _____

   _____

   _____

   _____

3. The customers' disappointment registers unmistakably. Because of its lost availability, the appliance suddenly becomes more attractive.

   _____

   _____

   _____

   _____

Writing Strategy: Outlining

Writing a simple outline is a good way not only to make sure you have understood the reading, but also a good way to organize notes to make sure you include the main ideas in a research paper or essay. Outlining also helps you prepare for tests because the most important ideas are compiled in one place. For example, a social science test may ask about a theory or principle—its definition and its effects. The sample outline would help you prepare to address questions on a test about the association principle.

1. Start with a very basic outline of the most important ideas. Look at this outline of the first reading:

    I. The association principle explains why sport fans are so devoted.
    II. People feel connected to others most like them.
    III. People want to be associated with successful sports teams in order to look good to others.
    IV. Similar associations exist outside of sports.

2. Add details and examples under the points they support. As a rough guide, each paragraph in a reading will correspond to either a main idea or a detail.

    <u>Note</u>: An outline contains ideas not just the order that information is presented in the reading. **Sometimes examples explain a preceding point, and sometimes they explain a point that follows.**

    I. The association principle explains why sport fans are so devoted.
        A. The bond between fans and their teams is very strong (silent soldier story).
        B. The bond is personal (silent soldier story).
    II. People feel connected to others most like them.
        A. They cheer for own gender, culture, or hometown.
        B. They distance themselves from failure.
    III. People want to be associated with successful sports teams in order to look good to others.
        A. They use *we* to feel closer to teams that are winning.
        B. They use *they* to distance themselves from teams that are losing.
    IV. Similar associations exist outside of sports.
        A. In politics: homeowners kept up signs of the winning party after elections.

It isn't necessary to write your outline in complete sentences or to include every detail. However, if your outline is too general, it will not offer you much help when you write or study for an exam.

Practice Activity: Outlining

Work with a partner to complete an outline for Reading 2. Follow the steps. Then write your outline on a separate piece of paper.

1. Create a basic outline of the main ideas.

2. Add details to each main point of your outline.

3. Add any examples in parentheses next to the detail they illustrate.

Your Active Vocabulary in the Real World

Vocabulary is important. Some words are useful for your speaking or for your writing, but other words are useful for your reading or your listening. For each word, decide how you think you will probably need this word for your English. Put a check mark (✓) under the correct ways you think you are likely to need the word. It is possible to have a check mark in more than one column.

	YOUR VOCABULARY	I need to be able to use this word in WRITING.	I need to be able to use this word in SPEAKING.	I need to understand this word in READING.	I need to understand this word in LISTENING.
1.	available				
2.	item				
3.	opportunity				
4.	possession				
5.	principle				
6.	rare				
7.	scarcity				
8.	valuable				
9.	vulnerable				
10.	worth				

Rapid Vocabulary Review

From the three answers on the right, circle the one that best explains, is an example of, or combines with vocabulary word on the left as it is used in this unit.

Vocabulary	Answers		
Synonyms			
1. puzzling	annoying	frightening	confusing
2. crucial	important	temporary	dangerous
3. a wound	an example	an argument	an injury
4. to shift	to create	to change	to cancel
5. flawed	has a good ending	has a mistake	has two possibilities
6. the outcome	the result	the ingredient	the middle part
7. likely	good-tasting	beautiful	probable
8. a concept	an idea	a statement	a plan
9. remove	take away	turn on	find out
10. an anecdote	a medicine	a family member	a story
11. a tactic	a dictionary	a plan	an application
12. for good	easily	permanently	occasionally
Combinations and Associations			
13. the bond ___ X and Y	between	for	on
14. a loyal ___	fan	orange	time
15. reveal the ___	eraser	answer	stress
16. ___ aware of something	takes	does	is
17. you're ___ to something	entitled	interested	surprised
18. ___ out the answer	think	discuss	figure
19. was ___ in something	angry	involved	wasted
20. was enhanced ___	at	for	by

⊏⋈⊐ Synthesizing: Writing Projects

In-Class Assignments	Outside Assignments
An Association	Olympic Ties
Describe something from your home-town, culture, or country with which you associate yourself, such as a sports team, school, or group of people. What are its characteristics? Do you feel you share any of the same characteristics? Give examples. **Suggested Length:** 300 words **Preparation:** none	Choose a famous Olympic athlete and describe how his/her career affected citizens of that country. You may choose someone who did well or who did poorly, or someone whose career had ups and downs. You can also choose a team. Give examples. **Suggested Length:** 800 words **Preparation:** Light research in a library or online
The Scarcity Principle	The Limited-Number Tactic in Action
Imagine you were taking a test in a psychology class. The instructor has given you an essay question. Write an essay that defines the scarcity principle and describes its causes and effects. Then choose an object whose value depends on scarcity that you do not think is worth what people will pay for it. Explain why you feel it is not actually valuable and why you think people want it or value it. Discuss why you would or would not like to own one. **Suggested Length:** 500 words **Preparation:** none	Visit an appliance or electronics store and show interest in a mid-range or inexpensive item. Ask a salesperson for advice. Find answers to questions like these: Does the salesperson use the limited-number tactic in any way? Does the store itself show any signs of using the limited-number tactic (for example, items on sale for a limited time)? Do you feel these tactics were persuasive? Why or why not? How did you personally respond to them? Were your responses different because of the reading in this unit? Discuss your results in a research report. **Suggested Length:** 1,000 words **Preparation:** Personal research in a store

Vocabulary Log

To increase your vocabulary knowledge, write a definition or translation for each vocabulary item. Then write an original phrase, sentence, or note that will help you remember the vocabulary item.

Vocabulary Item	Definition or Translation	Your Original Phrase, Sentence, or Note
1. detect	discover, find	detect a problem
2. grateful		
3. to notice		
4. set (something) aside		
5. wealthy		
6. make sense		
7. pervasive		
8. firmly		
9. superficial		
10. account for		
11. to damage		
12. a tendency		
13. in terms of		

Vocabulary Item	Definition or Translation	Your Original Phrase, Sentence, or Note
14. infiltrating		
15. enthusiastic		
16. compliance		
17. a switch		
18. vulnerable		
19. blurry		
20. distinguished (adj.)		
21. be prone to		
22. to disrupt		
23. particular		
24. never mind		
25. a fragment		

2 World Civilizations: Ancient Greece and Rome

Ancient Greek and Roman societies influenced much of Western philosophy, society, government, art, and sports. Modern Western countries study these societies to learn about their own origins and trace their development. The first reading examines some key differences between life in ancient Greece and Rome. The second reading makes a detailed comparison between the sport of chariot racing in the two civilizations.

Part 1: Differences between Ancient Greece and Rome

Getting Started

Famous Greek and Roman people, both real and mythological, are still studied in history courses today. Many common words in English come from Latin (the language of ancient Rome) or Greek and are still noticeable in modern English. The words appear as brand names, heroes, and even common words. Answer these questions with a partner.

1. Are you familiar with these Greek or Roman words: *atlas, Olympics, senator,* and *spartan?* Write a brief definition for each.

   _____

   _____

   _____

   _____

2. Nike was an ancient goddess and Hercules was a god. Can you guess what they represented based on their names? How are their names used today?

   _____

   _____

   _____

   _____

3. Sometimes you can figure out what the original Latin or Greek word meant by guessing the meaning of the word parts. Without using a dictionary, write a definition for each part of these words, and then write a definition for each word.

democracy	*demos* _____	*cracy* _____
_____		
peninsula	*pen* _____	*insula* _____
_____		
Mediterranean	*medi* _____	*terra* _____
_____		

Reading 1 is similar to what you might find in an encyclopedia or reference book. It's a general passage that describes two ancient civilizations, those of Rome and Greece, that are often thought to be similar. In spite of their similarities, however, there were many key differences.

In academic texts, you will often study two (or more) items, people, or events at the same time. Writers use **comparison** to point out similarities between things usually thought to be different and **contrast** to point out differences between two things usually thought to be similar. Reading 1 uses this particular organizational structure.

Before Reading Strategy: Developing a Purpose for Reading

Academic readings can be long and challenging. Sometimes it may be hard to motivate yourself to read, especially in a field that is different than your own. To combat this, it may help to develop a purpose for reading. In other words, **set a goal.** By working toward the goal, you will focus on the reading so you can achieve the goal. Always make sure that you know why you are reading the text and what information you need (or want) to learn.

Purposes can vary. It may be a purpose **from the teacher,** such as learning something that may appear later on a test or gathering information to complete a writing assignment. It may be a purpose **from the textbook,** such as a list of objectives at the beginning of the chapter. You may have to motivate yourself by asking questions about the topic that you hope to answer or questions you want to ask during a class discussion. You can also make predictions about the topic and then see how many you get right.

Setting goals helps you pay more attention to certain information. Focusing in this way helps you put more value on different parts of the reading rather than trying to remember every single detail.

Practice Activity: Developing a Purpose for Reading

Reading 1 is about the differences between ancient Greece and Rome. Focus on the topic by answering these questions.

1. What objectives does the instructor have for asking you to read this?

   _____

   _____

   _____

   _____

2. What differences between ancient Greece and Rome can you predict will be covered?

   _____

   _____

   _____

   _____

3. Why do you think the author chose to write about this topic? List at least two reasons.

   _____

   _____

   _____

   _____

During Reading Strategy: Making Text-to-World Connections

Successful academic readers are able to make connections between the text and the world. Doing this allows them to think about the topic and see the world a new way or consider the way another person may see it.

While you are reading, you should ask yourself what you already know about the topic, what it reminds you of, or what it makes you think about. In other words, connect the information in the reading to your life.

Make statements as you read such as:

> That reminds me of . . .
>
> I knew that, but I didn't know . . .
>
> That makes me wonder about . . .
>
> That sounds like an event I'm familiar with: the . . .
>
> If that were me, I would feel . . .
>
> I think that affects the world because . . .

For example, you may read:

> *Though it seems to do its utmost to be as ugly as possible, I still find Rome, the city I live in, very beautiful. Besides finding it so beautiful, I love it dearly and wouldn't leave it for anything in the world. Nevertheless, it has become quite difficult both to love it and to live in it, since these days it is a jungle of automobiles.*

Then you can make a text-to-world connection like:

> I knew Rome was beautiful because I've seen pictures, but I didn't know there were so many cars as to make it difficult to live there.

Making connections to the real world will help you better comprehend the material and help you maintain an interest because you can see its value beyond the text and how the topic may affect other people. Ask yourself what others may think about the topic or your opinion of the topic. You'll notice that what you know about something may grow or change as you read.

Practice Activity: Making Text-to-World Connections

Read each of these short passages, and then write a statement showing how you are making a connection between it and the real world. How can you relate to each statement? Then make text-to-world connections as you read Reading 1.

1. Why I yearned for Via Nizza I don't know. It was a street in my old neighborhood, but not the street where I grew up. And yet I would have given anything at all to be on Via Nizza, walking among its very tall buildings sealed with ice, breathing in its fog, its winter and melancholy.

   _____

   _____

2. A legend in his own time, Americans had been describing Washington as "the Father of the Country" since 1776—which is to say, before there was even a country.

   _____

   _____

3. Almost everyone is vulnerable to the scarcity principle in some form. Take as evidence the experience of Florida State University students who, like most undergraduates when surveyed, rated the quality of their campus cafeteria food unsatisfactory. Nine days later, according to a second survey, they had changed their minds. Something had happened to make them like their cafeteria's food significantly better than before.

   _____

   _____

4. A lot of strange behavior can be explained by the fact that people understand the association principle well enough to try to link themselves to positive events and separate themselves from negative events—even when they have not caused the events.

   _____

   _____

Vocabulary Power

There are a number of terms and phrases in this reading that you may encounter in other academic settings. Add at least five vocabulary items to your vocabulary note-book or log.

Match the words in bold from the reading on the left with a definition on the right.

1. _____ First, Greece never had a huge **empire** like Rome's.

2. _____ For example, when a group of Corinthians established the **colony** of Syracuse on the faraway island of Sicily, they did not think they were contributing to the growth of a Corinthian or Greek empire.

3. _____ They came, they **conquered**, they seized control.

4. _____ In both Greece and Rome, people were divided into social **classes**.

5. _____ Citizens could vote and even enter the government, regardless of who your **ancestors** were.

6. _____ They were taught to read and write and encouraged to **engage in** archery, races, and other physical contests.

7. _____ . . . a huge crowd of women gathered to force the **repeal** of a law that limited women's rights.

8. _____ Fortunately, archaeologists and scholars were able to recover many records and uncover numerous **artifacts**.

a. fought, won, and took over; beat

b. family members who lived long ago

c. take back or undo

d. goods or physical items, made by people; especially used to refer to those from previous civilizations

e. an area that may govern itself but has ties to another country

f. a group of countries or areas that is controlled by one government with significant power and influence

g. do; take part in

h. groups of people or populations who share similar characteristics

Reading

Now, read the passage. Make text-to-world connections as you read. Write notes or annotations in the margins.

Differences between Ancient Greece and Rome

(1) The civilizations of ancient Greece and Rome were similar in many ways. To modern eyes, Roman buildings look a lot like Greek buildings. Most gods in the Roman religion were simply Greek gods with new names. Romans hired Greek tutors to teach Greek culture to their children. These similarities, however, hide some important differences.

(2) First, Greece never had a huge empire like Rome's. Mountains and the sea separated Greeks into hundreds of communities called city-states, such as Athens, Sparta, and Corinth. Each had its own independent government. They shared a language and many aspects of culture, but they did not unite into a nation. An Athenian, for example, thought of Spartans or Corinthians as foreigners. When a group of Greeks established a new settlement a great distance from the others, it was not the expansion of a nation. It was not even the expansion of a city-state. For example, when a group of Corinthians established the colony of Syracuse on the faraway island of Sicily, they did not think they were contributing to the growth of a Corinthian or Greek empire. The colony expected to, and did, govern itself without depending on Corinth.

(3) Romans, on the other hand, enlarged their empire each time they took over a new land. They came, they conquered, and they seized control. Early in Rome's history, this empire-building was made easier because the Italian Peninsula terrain was not as rough as that in Greece, which was more mountainous.

(4) For example, officials could easily travel to a conquered Italian neighbor to apply Roman law and collect taxes. This pattern continued even as Rome conquered lands far from home. Even lands far away from the center of the Roman Empire were affected. Peoples from England to Egypt had to accept the rule of the Roman government and pay their taxes. As a result, Rome became very powerful.

(5) In both Greece and Rome, people were divided into social classes. In both societies, slaves and poor people lived at the bottom of the social ranks while rich people

The map shows the size of the Roman Empire around 117 ACE.

enjoyed life at the top. The Roman class system, however, was much more complicated than Greece's. In Greek city-states, not everyone could become a citizen. Only free males who owned property qualified. Once a male earned citizenship, though, he had the same rights and powers as any other. Citizens could vote and even enter the government, regardless of who their ancestors were.

(6) In Rome, however, family was everything. Even among citizens at the highest levels of society, known as patricians, there were differences. You could not become a Senator, a high government official, unless you were from a family of Senators. You could not be recognized as a nobleman (and only men could be noble) unless the last three generations of your family—your great-grandfather, grandfather, and father—were also nobles. Rome actually had officials, called censors, who might investigate the background of a well-known person. If the censors found that the person or his family did not perform enough honorable deeds, they could demote him to a lower class.

(7) Finally, the roles of women were very different in Rome and the Greek city-states. In one Greek city-state, Sparta, women had a great deal of freedom. Spartan men were tough warriors, and Spartan women were expected to be tough as well. They were taught to read and write and encouraged to engage in archery, races, and other physical

contests. In the other city-states, however, Greek women were expected to stay at home and take care of the family. They played no role in government, business, or any other public pursuit. Several Athenian writers—all men—portrayed women as inferior to men.

(8) The situation was different in Rome. According to tradition, the only women with a public position were the Vestal Virgins. They were responsible for keeping a sacred* fire burning. Other women, according to social rules, were expected to stay home and obey their husbands. In reality, however, the rules were not strictly followed. An ordinary woman had a lot of freedom and influence. Except for those of the lowest classes, women were well educated. Many husbands relied on them for advice and considered them partners. Women were free to go shopping, visit their friends, or otherwise travel alone. They also sometimes got involved in politics and public affairs. In 206 BCE†, a huge crowd of women gathered to force the repeal of a law that limited women's rights. They blocked streets and camped outside the houses of lawmakers. Eventually, the Roman Senate gave in and struck down* the law.

sacred: dedicated to worship of a god

struck down: forcefully removed something

(9) After the fall of the Roman Empire in about 400 ACE, a lot of learning and many cultural achievements were temporarily lost. Fortunately, archaeologists and scholars were able to recover many records and uncover numerous artifacts. They remind us that ancient Greece and Rome, different as they were, both had complex and diverse cultures, with much for us to admire.

†See page 56 for explanations of BCE and ACE.

Practice Activity: Reading for the Big Picture

Choose the best answer for each question.

1. What is the main idea of the passage?

   a. Roman society was considerably more advanced than Greek society.

   b. Although similar, Roman and Greek civilizations had some key differences in society and government.

   c. Artifacts provide essential clues to early Greek and Roman societies.

   d. It's important to study ancient Greece and Rome in order to learn from their examples in politics and social structure.

2. What was one main difference mentioned?

   a. buildings

   b. artifacts

   c. education

   d. size

After Reading Strategy: Organizing Information Based on Text Structure

After you have determined the text structure, you should organize your notes or annotations and information from the reading into a graphic organizer. In many cases, a chart will help you organize and comprehend the details. When two or more things are compared and contrasted in a reading, as they were in Reading 1, it can be useful to organize the similarities and differences. This will help you clarify which information is about which topic. Charts also make useful study aids before tests and class discussions and provide a useful outline for writing.

Practice Activity: Organizing Information Based on Text Structure

Complete the chart with information from the reading. Then compare charts with a partner. Make changes if you need to.

	only Greek	both Greek and Roman	only Roman
buildings		looked similar	
gods			
studied Greek culture			
empire			huge empire
landscape / geography	more mountainous		
social classes			
citizenship			
importance of family			
the role of women			

Paraphrasing to Simplify

Write a paraphrase that expresses the main points of the original without re-using too many words or phrases from the original.

1. In both societies, slaves and poor people lived at the bottom of the social ranks while rich people enjoyed life at the top.

   _____

   _____

   _____

   _____

2. Rome actually had officials, called censors, who might investigate the background of a well-known person.

   _____

   _____

   _____

   _____

3. After the fall of the Roman Empire in about 400 ACE, a lot of learning and many cultural achievements were temporarily lost.

   _____

   _____

   _____

   _____

Writing Strategy: Writing Compare and Contrast Essays

When you compare and contrast two or more topics (people, places, things, events, ideas, or any other items), it is important that the reader be able to tell which points are similar and which are different. There are several things you should do when you are writing a compare and contrast essay to help your audience.

First, use sentence patterns that make it clear to the reader that you are comparing or contrasting.

Comparing

Both the Greeks and the Romans were noted for . . .

The Greeks and Romans were similar in their ability to . . .

Like the Greeks, the Romans were important to history because . . .

Both the Greeks and the Romans shared . . .

Another aspect the Greeks and Romans had in common was . . .

Neither the Greeks nor the Romans enjoyed . . .

Contrasting

The Greeks and Romans had some key differences in . . .

The Greeks and Romans differed in . . .

Unlike the Greeks, the Romans were famous for . . .

In contrast to the Greeks, the Romans . . .

Another aspect in which they differed significantly was . . .

Second, include common signal words and phrases that compare and contrast.

Compare	Contrast
and	although
as	but
both	differs from
in the same way	even though
likewise	however
resembles	on the other hand
similarly	while
similar to	yet

Third, choose a good organizational pattern.

1. Block organization: Describe all of the first item, and then describe all of the second item.

2. Point-by-point organization: Describe one point of the first item and then the same point of the second item. Then describe the next point about the first and then the same point of the second item. Continue alternating until all points are described.

Block organization is ideal when there are not an equal number of points to compare and contrast about the two items or when the direct similarities and differences between the two are not the main idea of the whole paper. Point-by-point organization is more common when you need to emphasize certain similarities or differences.

Practice Activity: Writing Compare and Contrast Statements

1. Using signal words and phrases on page 50, write sentences that compare these areas of Greek and Roman civilizations:

   a. buildings

   _____

   _____

   b. religion

   _____

   _____

   c. social classes

   _____

   _____

2. Using signal words and phrases on page 50, write sentences that contrast these areas of Greek and Roman civilizations:

   a. landscape / geography

   _____

   _____

   b. citizenship

   _____

   _____

   c. the role of women

   _____

   _____

3. Now imagine you have to answer an essay question on an exam. Write a general topic sentence to summarize the main idea of Reading 1.

   _____

   _____

   _____

   _____

Short Writing Tasks

Write your response to each task following the directions given for length and source material.

Task 1 (Summary)

Look again at Reading 1. Write a one-paragraph summary of the reading. Do not simply copy from the reading. A suggested approach is to make a list of key words and main ideas from the reading and then to not look at the reading again. Review the box on page 15. Use only your notes as you prepare your own summary. Be sure to mention or cite your source. (Length: 5–7 sentences)

_____

_____

_____

_____

_____

_____

_____

Task 2 (Research)

Reading 1 discusses two ancient civilizations that strongly influenced Western culture. Based on your instructor's guidelines, do some light research online or in a library to find another item, word, activity, or idea of Greek or Roman origin. State what you chose, and describe how it is used in today's modern world and how it has changed from its original use. Take notes in the space provided. Then write your paragraph on a separate piece of paper. (Length: 5–7 sentences)

_____

_____

_____

_____

_____

_____

_____

Part 2: Greek and Roman Chariot Racing

Getting Started

Many—if not most—of the sports people enjoy today originated in ancient times. Some sports, however, are not as popular as they once were, or perhaps they have evolved into different forms of the sport. For example, some sports are only seen in movies such as *Spartacus* or *Gladiator*, but are no longer played today. No matter what the sport, one thing they seemed to have in common was the type of place they were played. Sporting competitions in the ancient world were held in public areas where people could watch and support their favorite teams. The same is true today with professional sports teams playing in large arenas and stadiums with thousands of fans gathering for the games. Answer these questions with a partner.

1. What kinds of races or sports do people commonly participate in today? times? What kinds have you participated in? What kinds have you watched?

   _____

   _____

   _____

   _____

2. What are some reasons that people compete in races or sports? What are some reasons that people watch others compete?

   _____

   _____

   _____

   _____

3. Think of a few sporting events that are popular in your culture. Do you think an interest in these sports indicates any cultural values of the people who play or watch? If so, which ones?

   _____

   _____

   _____

   _____

Reading 2, from the history textbook *Life, Death, and Entertainment in the Roman Empire,* discusses the sport of chariot racing, which was popular in ancient Greek and Roman times. Horses pulled small carts, called chariots, in which one or more men stood, guiding the horses. The arena in which they raced was called a *circus* (for its circular or oval shape), from which we get the modern English word *circus,* meaning a special type of entertainment or show that takes place in an arena.

These sporting events were popular and are documented in literature and in modern film. Homer, a poet from ancient Greece, wrote the *Iliad. The Iliad* is an epic poem set during the Trojan War and tells stories of the battles and events during that time in Greek history, including a sporting event—a chariot race—between two characters.

When reading about historical events, it is important to be able to understand the time frame discussed in the text.

Before Reading Strategy: Understanding Chronology

When you read academic works, you will encounter dates and time periods. It is not difficult to locate these in a text; you will notice them when you skim the text. Some terms and abbreviations are common in academic texts discussing history.

BC = *before Christ*; before the birth of Jesus Christ in the Christian calendar

BCE = *before the Common Era*: a more modern term for BC

AD = *anno domini*, Latin for *in the year of our Lord*; after the birth of Jesus Christ in the Christian calendar

ACE = *after the Common Era*: a more modern term for AD

Knowing the dates helps you get a sense of the context. Whenever you see a date, year, or chronology word, follow these steps.

1. Contextualize the dates, years, and chronology words for yourself so that you can understand their significance. *What does 20,000 years ago mean? Were humans alive then? What does 1957 mean? Had television been invented? Had the Internet?*

2. For items that are not easy for you to contextualize, take a few moments to check a timeline online or in a reference book. This helps you get a sense of why the topic was important. *What major world events am I familiar with that were happening at that time?*

3. Pay attention to words that indicate lengths of time, such as *day, week, month, year, decade* (10 years), and *century* (100 years). *Can the length of time be equated to any events in my life?*

4. The numbers may seem confusing, but remember that a century is 100 years and that the first century began in year 1. The 16th century, for example, refers to events from 1500 to 1599.

Practice Activity: Understanding Chronology

Scan for the dates mentioned in the paragraphs listed. Write them in the space provided. Then talk with a partner about what the world was like at that time. What was happening? If you are not sure, check another source to find out.

1. Paragraph 4:

    a. _____

    b. _____

    c. _____

2. Paragraph 5: _____

3. Paragraph 9: _____

    a. _____

    b. _____

During Reading Strategy: Making Text-to-Text Connections

For Reading 1, you learned that making text-to-world connections improves your comprehension and helps you think broadly about the topic. Successful academic readers are also able to make text-to-text connections. This is especially helpful in academic study because you will often have to write papers or essays or answer exam questions about two readings or sources.

While you are reading, it is important to connect two specific readings or connect one reading to another reading you have read before. This is helpful because you are then thinking about the topic and what the readings have in common or how they differ. You can also compare people, actions, settings, or time periods.

Make statements as you read such as:

This reading reminds me of another because . . .

This reading is similar to the other reading because in both, [this] happens. . .

This reading differs from the first one since . . .

These readings are alike in . . .

I knew this because I read about it in . . .

That's familiar because I read about it in . . .

For example, you may read:

A circus, the arena for chariot racing, was the largest public building in the Roman world, and under the emperors it had become the central location for communication between the emperor and his people.

You can make a text-to-text connection with Reading 1 like:

This reading reminds me of Reading 1 because it also gave a lot of information about life during the Roman empire. I now have a picture in my head of life then.

Making connections between texts will help you review the earlier readings, and drawing comparisons and noticing contrasts will be useful when taking tests, writing essays, or doing research for papers.

Practice Activity: Making Text-to-Text Connections

Read each of these short passages from Reading 2, and write a statement showing how you are making a connection from it to Reading 1. Then make connections to other texts with which you are familiar as you read Reading 2. You can make connections by annotating the connections in the margin of the readings.

1. The earliest description of a chariot race is in the 23rd book of Homer's *Iliad*, where it appears as the main event at the funeral games for Achilles' deceased friend Patroclus. In the *Iliad*, which probably reflects the style of chariot racing that was current in eighth-century Greece. . . .

   _____

   _____

   _____

   _____

2. Chariot grounds from ancient Greece are not easy to locate. This is because in the Greek system, a flat plain was a sufficient condition for a race.

   _____

   _____

   _____

   _____

3. One of the most important aspects of Greek chariot racing is that it ordinarily remained outside the structures of civic athleticism. Although there is some evidence for cities sponsoring teams, teams and drivers were usually provided by aristocrats who wanted to participate in the sport.

   _____

   _____

   _____

   _____

Vocabulary Power

There are a number of terms and phrases in this reading that you may encounter in other academic settings. Add at least five vocabulary items to your vocabulary notebook or log.

Match the words in bold from the reading on the left with a definition on the right.

1. _____ Although there is some evidence for cities **sponsoring** teams, teams and drivers were usually provided by aristocrats who wanted to participate in the sport.

2. _____ One of the most important aspects of Greek chariot racing is that it ordinarily remained outside the structures of **civic** athleticism.

3. _____ It was very difficult for chariots to pass each other, and the ability to force an **opponent** to take a slightly longer course could be a crucial factor in a race.

4. _____ The counterclockwise turn is characteristic of all chariot races in the Mediterranean world, where it was **assumed** that charioteers would be right-handed.

5. _____ That is to the advantage of the **spectators**, who would be inconvenienced if the chariots dashed off out of sight.

6. _____ Even a **slight** difference in position with regard to the turning post could have an impact on the race.

7. _____ We know very little about chariot racing in Italy **prior to** the emergence of a set race-course in the Circus Maximus at Rome.

8. _____ A circus was one of the most **prestigious** buildings, marking its host city as a center of power.

a. before

b. someone competing against another in a sport, battle, contest, or difficult situation

c. of high status; important

d. small

e. taken or believed to be true

f. about a city; relating to the functions or government of a city

g. paying for

h. people who watch a performance

Reading

Now, read this passage. Make text-to-text connections as you read. Write notes or annotations in the margins.

Public Entertainment in Rome and Greece

(1) A circus, the arena for chariot racing, was the largest public building in the Roman world, and under the emperors it had become the central location for communication between the emperor and his people.

(2) Circus buildings were comparatively rare (fewer than one hundred) even in the third century. A circus was one of the most prestigious buildings, marking its host city as a center of power. It is important to realize that the Roman form of circus chariot racing evolved in a purely Roman context. There were other forms of chariot racing in the Mediterranean world, and the Roman variety was determined by the shape of the racing ground at the Circus Maximus, which ultimately provided a model for the other circuses; the organization of the event, with chariots fielded by four professional factions (known as stables), was also, as far as we know, a unique development by the city of Rome.

Greek Chariot Racing

(3) People other than Romans raced chariots, and they had done so for centuries prior to the Roman conquest of the Mediterranean. These races differed in various ways from the seven laps around a long, low barrier that characterized Roman races. The earliest description of a chariot race is in the 23rd book of Homer's *Iliad*,

The Appian Way

where it appears as the main event at the funeral games for Achilles' deceased friend Patroclus. In the *Iliad*, which probably reflects the style of chariot racing that was current in eighth-century Greece, a group of heroes drives four-horse chariots over a flat plain to a turning post marked by two white stones and a judge. They pass around the turning post and race back to the starting line. The key features of this event are that the heroes are out for themselves, supplying their own teams and driving the teams themselves; the ground has not been specially prepared for the race; there are no permanent seats; and the contestants race around a turning post in a counterclockwise direction. The use of a turning post makes for a longer race and a more economical use of space. That is to the advantage of spectators, who would be inconvenienced if the chariots dashed off out of sight. The counterclockwise turn is characteristic of all chariot races in the Mediterranean world, where it was assumed that charioteers would be right-handed. Other factors of interest are the stones, which help prevent the chariots from running into the turning post and the judge. Even in the heroic age, steps had to be taken to prevent cheating. Finally, Homer's heroes drew lots* to determine their starting positions. Even a slight difference in position with regard to the turning post could have an impact on the race. It was very difficult for

drew lots: determined by choosing something by chance

chariots to pass each other, and the ability to force an opponent to take a slightly longer course could be a critical factor in a race.

(4) Chariot grounds from ancient Greece are not easy to locate. This is because in the Greek system, a flat plain was a sufficient condition for a race. Even starting gates were rare. The absence of permanent starting mechanisms may be due to the fact that the number of contestants was not predictable: there is evidence that as many as 41 chariots took part in a single race at Delphi in the third century BCE. It is only at Olympia that we get evidence for a regular starting mechanism, and here there was a provision for as many as 48 teams. In the fifth century BCE, a mechanism was finally constructed to permit a staggered start, so that the teams that were furthest from the turning post left the gates before those that were closest. The fifth century date for the construction of this mechanism, which seems to have been modeled on the mechanism used for footraces, is significant. The first attested Olympic chariot race was in 680 BCE, yet mechanisms and race courses were absent in most of mainland Greece and this suggests a certain level of amateurism.

(5) One of the most important aspects of Greek chariot racing is that it ordinarily remained outside the structures of civic athleticism. Although there is some evidence for

cities sponsoring teams, teams and drivers were usually provided by aristocrats*
who wanted to participate in the sport. These aristocratic participants were
interested in their own glory. As early as the sixth century BCE, there is
evidence that the glory to the aristocrat who financed a successful team at
one of the Panhellenic festivals was very important.

aristocrats: members of a high class of society; often wealthy and important

(**6**) The key organizational features of Greek chariot racing were as follows:

1. It was an activity for the very wealthy.
2. There could be a very large number of teams in each race.
3. There was very little permanent construction associated with the racetrack.

Chariot Racing in Italy

(**7**) We know very little about chariot racing in Italy prior to the emergence of a set
racecourse in the Circus Maximus at Rome. On the basis of Etruscan* tomb
paintings and some relief sculpture,* we know that the Etruscans appear to
have held chariot (and horse) races in the same arenas that were used for some
other athletic contests. We can see that they could erect temporary wooden
stands for these events, and it appears that seating was determined by class.
The racecourses had posts at the end opposite the starting line, but we cannot be
absolutely certain that chariots turned around these posts. They could mark a finish line.

Etruscan: ancient Italian civilization

relief sculpture: a type of artwork in which the forms are raised from the surface

(**8**) The basic features of the Circus Maximus were as follows:

1. Chariots were raced in multiples of four (but never more than twelve at a time).
2. The chariots were provided by four professional stables that were identified by color (the Blue, Green, Red, and White factions).
3. Chariots started from gates (carceres).
4. There were two turning posts, around which the chariots raced seven times.
5. There was a sprint from the starting gates to the first turning post.
6. The teams ran in a counterclockwise direction around the turning posts.
7. The finish line was in the middle of the track.

(9) The Circus Maximus, the only known location in early Rome where chariots were raced, is a flat space between two hills. The earliest date for building in this area is provided by the Augustinian historian Livy, who says that Rome's fifth king, Tarquinius Priscus, built seats in what was an urban area. Dionysus of Halicarnassus (another Augustan historian) says that Tarquinius' grandson—also named Tarquinius—who was also the last king of Rome, completed the work there. The traditional dates for Tarquinius Priscus, 616–575 BCE, are based on guesses (some would say that the same is true of Tarquinius himself), but the younger Tarquinius Priscus was almost certainly a real person, and the regal period appears to have ended between 509 and 500 BCE. The belief that the younger Tarquinius built stands in the Circus Maximus suggests that the Romans thought that a racecourse was laid out before the beginning of the Republic, and this is possible. What is exceptional about this project as an act of urban planning is that the racecourse was placed inside the settled urban area, according to Humphrey in *Roman Circuses: Arenas for Chariot Racing* (1986, pp. 60–61).

After Reading Strategy: Drawing Conclusions

Often writers will directly state what they want you to know. They will tell you the conclusions to be drawn from the facts and examples they used. However, sometimes the conclusion is left unstated, and the reader is expected to draw his or her own conclusions from the evidence presented.

1. If a paragraph or section doesn't end with a stated conclusion, ask yourself questions such as, *What is the importance of this? What do these examples mean about the topic? Why did the writer choose to tell me these things?*

2. It may be helpful to re-read topic sentences in the final paragraphs or the introduction of a section. The writer may have stated the purpose of the passage in these sections.

3. If you can't figure out a conclusion immediately, continue reading. Perhaps you will be able to draw a conclusion after a few more paragraphs. However, if that doesn't help, it's possible that you haven't totally understood what you have read. Check unfamiliar words in a dictionary or talk with a classmate about the meaning of the passage.

4. Be careful, of course, not to draw conclusions that are not supported with evidence in the text. You must be able to state not only what you think the passage implies, but also why you think so.

Practice Activity: Drawing Conclusions

Circle the letter of the best conclusion. Then share your answers with a partner. Say why you think the other conclusions are not as strong.

1. The use of a turning post makes for a longer race and a more economical use of space. That is to the advantage of spectators, who would be inconvenienced if the chariots dashed off out of sight.

   a. Audience involvement and reaction was important to chariot racers.

   b. Before the invention of turning posts, spectators weren't interested in watching chariot races.

   c. Chariot racers would have preferred to have a completely straight race course.

2. Finally, Homer's heroes drew lots to determine their starting positions. Even a slight difference in position with regard to the turning post could have an impact on the race.

   a. To the ancient Greeks, having an equal chance for an advantageous position was seen as fair.

   b. The Greeks didn't mind that chariot racing was a sport of luck, not a sport of skill.

   c. Drawing lots to determine starting positions happened only in fiction, such as in Homer's stories, not in actual races.

3. The counterclockwise turn is characteristic of all chariot races in the Mediterranean world, where it was assumed that charioteers would be right-handed.

   a. Left-handed charioteers would not have been able to win a race, so it is likely that they didn't bother to compete.

   b. Horses prefer to race in a counterclockwise direction.

   c. If you are right-handed, it is easier to turn a chariot to the right than to the left.

Write a conclusion that can be drawn from the sentences. Then compare your answers with a partner.

4. We know very little about chariot racing in Italy prior to the emergence of a set racecourse in the Circus Maximus at Rome.

_____

_____

5. The traditional dates for Tarquinius Priscus, 616–575 BCE, are based on guesses (some would say that the same is true of Tarquinius himself), but the younger Tarquinius Priscus was almost certainly a real person, and the regal period appears to have ended between 509 and 500 BCE.

_____

_____

Practice Activity: Reading for the Big Picture

Write T if the statement is true or F if the statement is false.

1. _____ Chariot racing as a sport was first developed in Rome.

2. _____ It's difficult to determine dates for chariot racing because it's hard to find artifacts or evidence from the sport.

3. _____ Greek chariot racing was a sport sponsored by artistocrats.

4. _____ Roman chariot races featured fewer chariots racing at one time than Greek races.

Paraphrasing to Simplify

Write a paraphrase that expresses the main points of the original without re-using too many words or phrases from the original.

1. One of the most important aspects of Greek chariot racing is that it ordinarily remained outside the structures of civic athleticism.

   _____

   _____

   _____

   _____

2. The racecourses have posts at the end opposite the starting line, but we cannot be absolutely certain that chariots turned around these posts.

   _____

   _____

   _____

   _____

3. What is exceptional about this project as an act of urban planning is that the racecourse was placed inside the settled urban area.

   _____

   _____

   _____

   _____

Writing Strategy: Revising

When you are taking an exam or writing an academic essay or paper, it is necessary to schedule time for revising. During your revision, your goal is to make the overall work stronger. There are several things you should check when you are revising.

1. Content: Make sure all your content is accurate, relates to the topic, and is easy to understand.

2. Goal: Ensure you are answering the instructor's question or prompt or are achieving the purpose of your paper.

3. Grammar: Check sentence structure and other grammatical issues such as verb tenses, agreement, plurals, and articles.

4. Punctuation: Edit to make sure you are following punctuation rules for periods, commas, semi-colons, and other punctuation marks.

5. Spelling: Re-read handwritten work or use a spell checker, and correct any misspelled words.

Although this process can be time-consuming, it ensures that you will turn in a stronger piece of writing.

Practice Activity: Revising

Read this paragraph. Revise it using numbers 3–5 from the box to make it a better piece of writing. Compare your ideas for revision with a partner.

Naturalists and hunters who have studied the behavior of herds of wild animals, including caribou and elks, have often observed that the herds can get alarmed and flee after one member senses danger. In some cases this can be explained in term of sensory signals. In other cases observers are often at a loss to explain the sudden flight of animals that shorty before, under the same circumstances, were feeding or rest without suspision. A sense of danger or alarm can spread silent and rapidly.

Now, revise one of your short writing tasks from Part 1 on page 53. Exchange your paper with a partner, and make suggestions for revisions for each other. Then re-write your assignment.

Your Active Vocabulary in the Real World

Vocabulary is important. Some words are useful for your speaking or for your writing, but other words are useful for your reading or your listening. For each word, decide how you think you will probably need this word for your English. Put a check mark (✓) under the correct ways you think you are likely to need the word. It is possible to have a check mark in more than one column.

	YOUR VOCABULARY	I need to be able to use this word in WRITING.	I need to be able to use this word in SPEAKING.	I need to understand this word in READING.	I need to understand this word in LISTENING.
1.	ancient				
2.	chariot				
3.	civic				
4.	empire				
5.	event				
6.	features				
7.	gave in				
8.	opponents				
9.	power				
10.	racing				

Rapid Vocabulary Review

From the three answers on the right, circle the one that best explains, is an example of, or combines with vocabulary word on the left as it is used in this unit.

Vocabulary	Answers		
Synonyms			
1. evidence	theories	proof	hope
2. tough	almost	careful	difficult
3. major	very important	very negative	very serious
4. slight	little	open	rough
5. similar	different	intelligent	like
6. plain	simple	ugly	vicious
7. require	know	need	persuade
8. permanent	never	sometimes	always
9. complex	complicated	honest	quiet
10. ancient	very angry	very light	very old
11. essential	farther	necessary	surprised
12. mention	say, tell	know, learn	burst, explode
Combinations and Associations			
13. a forest	a group of animals	a group of trees	a group of universities
14. ____ well	as	for	these
15. portray	a pilot	a taxi driver	a movie actor
16. huge	a mosquito	a whale	a mouse
17. a brand	a cat's lifetime	a company's name	a friend's information
18. exceptional	snow in a jungle	sand in a desert	fish in a lake
19. noticeable	a pen in an office	a small insect	a cut on your face
20. faraway	a place	a flight	a neighbor

⇨⇦ Synthesizing: Writing Projects

In-Class Assignments	Outside Assignments
The Importance of History	Famous Races
Explain the meaning of this quote: *Those who do not study the past are doomed to repeat it.* Then give your personal reaction. Do you agree or disagree with it? Support your opinion with examples. **Suggested Length:** 300 words **Preparation:** none	Choose *one* of these types of races. Explain the event, how and when it began, and how common it is today. Has the form of the race changed? Use chronology words as needed. a. the triathlon b. the decathlon c. the marathon **Suggested Length:** 800 words **Preparation:** Light research in a library or online
Sports Now and Then	Online Research: The Influence of Greek and Roman Mythology in Advertising
Imagine you have to take an essay exam in your history class. Write a compare and contrast essay between sporting events today and sporting events in ancient times using the readings in this unit. Use appropriate sentence structure, signal words and phrases, and organizational patterns. Take time to revise. **Suggested Length:** 500 words **Preparation:** none	Research online to discover some popular symbols of and characters from Greek and Roman mythology (for example, Pegasus the flying horse). In what store and brand names can you find references to these symbols and characters? You may refer to both words and pictures. If possible, include graphics in your essay. List your results, and explain why you think these companies chose these symbols or characters for their business. **Suggested Length:** 1,000 words **Preparation:** Light research in a library or online; personal observation outside the classroom

Vocabulary Log

To increase your vocabulary knowledge, write a definition or translation for each vocabulary item. Then write an original phrase, sentence, or note that will help you remember the vocabulary item.

Vocabulary Item	Definition or Translation	Your Original Phrase, Sentence, or Note
1. fancy	not plain	a very fancy car
2. race		
3. effort		
4. a series of		
5. draw a conclusion		
6. permanent		
7. with regard to		
8. original		
9. get involved in		
10. an event		
11. hold a race		
12. follow a step		
13. participate in		
14. determine		

Vocabulary Item	Definition or Translation	Your Original Phrase, Sentence, or Note
15. urban		
16. a variety of		
17. recover		
18. enlarge		
19. point out		
20. major (adjective)		
21. effort		
22. contrast		
23. associate with		
24. items		
25. mechanism		

3 Astronomy: Studying Space

Astronomy is the study of space. Astronomers study stars, planets, and other objects in the solar system and beyond. The first reading in this unit is about Pluto, which had been considered a planet, but when a new definition of the word *planet* was established in 2006, people said that Pluto was not a planet. The second reading is about the famous Hubble Telescope and how it works.

Part 1: Pluto: A Planet or Not a Planet?

Getting Started

Many people know very little about space. However, most people have studied something about the solar system and its planets before. Answer these questions with a partner.

1. When did you first study planets and the solar system? What did you learn about them?

_____

_____

_____

2. What else do you know about objects in space or theories about space? How did you learn these things?

_____

_____

_____

3. What kinds of space exploration and discoveries do you think will take place in the future? What questions do you think might be answered in your lifetime?

_____

_____

_____

Reading 1 is about Pluto. As the title suggests, Pluto was once considered a planet, but it is not any longer. This reading will give you some background on the history of our understanding of Pluto, and it will explain why a group of scientists decided in 2006 that it is not actually a planet.

Before reading a passage, it can be helpful to predict what you might learn. It doesn't matter if your predictions are wrong because your goal is to focus on the topic. Even incorrect predictions will improve your comprehension.

Before Reading Strategy: Predicting

Making some predictions before you read a text is a beneficial and common pre-reading strategy. In some ways, it may seem similar to activating prior knowledge, but it's different. It's different because even if you don't know anything about the topic, you can predict what you might find in the reading.

When you **predict,** you use the information you've been given, such as the title, to get some idea about the topic just to prepare you for what you might read. For example, you know this is a unit on the discipline of Astronomy, so you can make some predictions about what the reading will be about just based on that information. Once you know that, you can start to think about vocabulary that you know that is related to astronomy as well as any concepts you might be aware of—things like space as a concept or something space-related in the news (activity at the international space station). In terms of vocabulary, you should begin to ask yourself which words you already know, such as *planet* or *satellite*.

Practice Activity: Predicting

Look at the title and illustration on page 81. Then answer the questions. Do <u>not</u> read Reading 1 yet.

1. What is this reading going to be about, and what perspective is taken on the topic?

   _____

   _____

2. List six vocabulary items (words or phrases) that you predict you will find in a reading on this topic.

   _____

   _____

   _____

3. What other predictions do you want to make about the contents of the reading?

   _____

   _____

During Reading Strategy: Understanding Glosses

Language learning textbooks often feature glosses in readings to help students with vocabulary or with other information with which the reader may not be familiar. Glosses typically provide definitions or synonyms of vocabulary items (words or phrases) and appear in the margin, at the bottom of a page, or at the end of a reading. Note the glosses you have seen in the margins of the readings in Units 1 and 2.

Sometimes glosses provide more of an explanation of a phrase or concept. For example, in an excerpt from an older text, say from 1860, the writer may have made reference to something that was commonly known at the time of the writing but that would be an obscure reference for today's readers. In that case, a gloss or explanatory note would provide modern-day readers with the information they need to understand the text. In these cases, the gloss is provided more to help with comprehension of the text than to just understanding some of the vocabulary.

You should not stop reading when you encounter a word that is glossed. Glosses are most helpful if you follow a procedure.

1. When you notice that a word or phrase is glossed, finish reading the sentence first.

2. Go back and read the sentence up to the glossed word and then read the information in the gloss—the definition, synonym, or explanation. Even if the gloss is provided at the end of the reading, you should read it before you finish reading the text.

3. Go back and re-read the sentence in full this time. Check your understanding now that you have read the gloss.

4. Then finish reading the text or continue to the next word that is glossed.

Reading a text with glosses may take you more time, but it's worth it to make sure you understand the vocabulary or reading as a whole.

Practice Activity: Understanding Glosses

Answer the questions about glosses.

1. Look at the glosses in the readings in Units 1 and 2. How many glosses are about vocabulary? Which ones?

   _____

   _____

   _____

2. How many are explanatory notes? Which ones?

   _____

   _____

   _____

As you read about Pluto in Reading 1, follow the steps listed in the box on page 78, and then answer the questions each time you come to a gloss.

3. How many of the glosses provide definitions of vocabulary or synonyms? Which ones?

   _____

   _____

   _____

   _____

4. How many of the glosses explain a concept or piece of cultural information? Which ones?

   _____

   _____

   _____

   _____

Vocabulary Power

There are a number of terms and phrases in this lecture that you may encounter in other academic settings. Add at least five vocabulary items to your vocabulary notebook or log.

Match the words in bold from the reading on the left with a definition on the right.

1. _____ Eventually, scientists decided Pluto was just too unusual and they removed it from the **exclusive** club of what people consider to be the major planets.

2. _____ These characteristics **qualified** it to be a planet.

3. _____ It **dominates** its "neighborhood" in space by pulling smaller objects either into it or around it as moons.

4. _____ Astronomers now know that no **mysterious** body pulls it off course.

5. _____ The solar system now can only **boast** eight planets and Pluto has been redefined as a dwarf or minor planet.

6. _____ Pluto qualifies according to the first two **criteria**.

7. _____ Pluto was now obviously smaller than other objects being discovered at the far **reaches** of the solar system.

8. _____ The matter was **eventually** settled by an the IAU at its annual convention in 2006.

a. standards on which decisions are made

b. curious, having no reason

c. edges, borders

d. limited, not including others

e. finally

f. has control or a prominent place

g. claim or call attention to something, be proud of

h. met the requirements of

Reading

Now, read the passage, and follow the procedure for understanding glosses as you read.

Pluto: A Planet No More

(1) In August of 2006, our solar_system lost a planet. Until then, astronomers counted nine planets orbiting the Sun. The farthest one was Pluto, a cold body of rock and ice. It was so distant that the Sun was a mere dot in the Plutonian sky. It had extremely unusual characteristics, including an orbit that occasionally brought it closer to the Sun than Neptune, the planet that was furthest away until Pluto's discovery. Pluto's moons did not orbit the planet itself. Additionally, its rock-and-ice body made it more like a comet than a planet. Eventually, scientists decided Pluto was just too unusual, and they removed it from the exclusive club of what people consider to be the major planets.

(2) Pluto's discovery in 1930 caused a wealth of excitement among astronomers and non-scientists alike. The son of a wealthy aristocratic family, Percival Lowell, was committed to discovering new astronomical wonders, including water on Mars. He also sought Planet X, an unseen object that he suspected was guilty of pulling planet Uranus. His efforts also resulted in the founding of the Lowell Observatory* in 1894. When Pluto was discovered, it seemed that the mysterious Planet X that Lowell had hunted had been captured. Unfortunately, Lowell died in 1916 and didn't see his suspicions come to fruition.* Excited people worldwide suggested names for the newly discovered body.

Lowell Observatory: a private institution committed to research and public outreach

come to fruition: be realized, happen

(3) It was actually a man named Clyde Tombaugh who discovered Pluto. Tombaugh's beginnings in astronomy stem from a telescope he built himself, which he used to scan the night skies. In 1927, he sent drawings of the skies he witnessed to

Lowell Observatory. His hope was simply to get feedback on his work. However, the astronomers did more than that; they hired him to photograph the skies. By scanning photographic plates of the same area of the night sky for differences, Tombaugh noticed one speck of light moving, as a planet would, in January of 1930. By March, the discovery of the ninth planet was announced, and Tombaugh skyrocketed to stardom himself. Although he had entered Lowell with only a high school education, the honors of discovering a planet spurred him to finish a university education and complete his graduate work. Tombaugh's work didn't end there. After he founded the Astronomy Department at New Mexico State University, his number of discoveries kept growing. He has been credited with discovering a comet,* a nova,* several open clusters, a globular cluster, and a supercluster of galaxies.

comet: a space body with a head and tail that has an unusual orbit

nova: a star that suddenly gets very bright and then fades away after time

(4) The name Pluto, which was the name of the Roman god of the underworld, was suggested by an 11-year-old British girl and followed the tradition of naming planets after Greek or Roman gods (not, as some people think, after the Disney character). Although the name is fitting for a planet so far removed from the Sun, it is also fitting that its first two letters are the same as the initials of Percival Lowell. Today, naming rights of any astrological body belong to an organization called the International Astronomers Union (IAU).

(5) Astronomers knew very little about Pluto. They guessed that it was large and heavy enough to affect Uranus's orbit and that it appeared to be round. These characteristics qualified it to be a planet. However, as space observation became more exact in the late 20th century, doubts began to surface. Pluto's largest moon, Charon, was discovered in 1978, and its movements showed Pluto to be much smaller than anyone thought. Until then, Pluto's size was assumed to be larger than Mercury, the planet closest to the Sun. To compound the doubts, Pluto was also no longer the only object beyond Neptune as it had been when originally discovered. In fact, a multitude of other objects comprised of the same rock and ice had been discovered. Pluto was now obviously smaller than other objects being discovered at the far reaches of the solar system. This was a problem. Should astronomers count all these objects as new planets? If not, how could it be fair for Pluto to be a planet when larger objects were not?

(6) The matter was eventually settled by the IAU at its annual convention in 2006. The IAU officially defined a planet as having all three of these characteristics:

1. It is massive enough to become approximately round, thanks to the pull of its own gravity.
2. It independently orbits the Sun.
3. It dominates its "neighborhood" in space by pulling smaller objects either into it or around it as moons.

(7) Pluto qualifies according to the first two criteria. It definitely orbits the Sun, completing its journey every 248 Earth years. It is also generally round. However, many other space objects also have these characteristics. For example, in 2005 another body beyond Neptune, called Eris, was discovered and found to be larger than Pluto. It is round. It orbits the Sun. Pluto's planethood made no sense if an object like Eris was considered less than a planet.

(8) Pluto fails, however, to make the cut because its mass is too low to dominate its neighborhood. It travels in a part of the solar system called the Kuiper Belt, which is full of space rocks and chunks of ice. Pluto's gravity is not strong enough to control the paths of the pieces in this disorganized collection of debris. Pluto was once thought to have three moons—a large, nearby one called Charon and two farther out called Nix and Hydra. It now appears that none of these three actually orbits Pluto. Instead, they all—including

Pluto itself—orbit an empty point in space that lies between Pluto and Charon. Even Pluto's role as Lowell's Planet X has been proven false. New measurements of Uranus's orbit show it to be normal. Astronomers now know that no mysterious body pulls it off course. Therefore, according to these details, Pluto is not domineering.

(9) The IAU now considers Pluto and at least 44 other objects, including Charon and Eris, minor or dwarf planets, and minor planets and "regular" planets are two very distinct categories to the IAU. The minor planets are not even considered a subcategory because this would force the IAU to include more than a few planets into the solar system, so that proposal was eventually dropped. Some scientists disagree with the IAU and continue to say that there are nine planets in our solar system. Their position, however, becomes harder to support as more and more Kuiper Belt objects larger than Pluto are discovered. According to the definitions drafted in 2006, a "dwarf" planet is one that is in orbit and has enough mass for its own gravity to assume a round shape but does not dominate its neighborhood. Therefore, Pluto is absolutely not a planet. The solar system now can only boast eight planets, and Pluto has been redefined as a dwarf or minor planet. Planet Pluto enjoyed 76 years of fame, and Tombaugh, who lived until 1997, never knew that his discovery was not truly that of another planet. Right or wrong, both Pluto and Tombaugh have been demoted.

After Reading Strategy: Deciding If the Author's Purpose Was Accomplished

Unit 2 discussed how determining the purpose of a reading is an important strategy before reading. Purpose also plays an important role after reading a passage.

Authors have a purpose for everything that they write, but sometimes, it's harder than it should be to discover the purpose. Sometimes it can be clear what the purpose is when you start a reading but less clear when you finish. As a result, it's important to take a minute to think about a reading when you finish it to discover if you think the purpose was met by the author. In other words, did the author accomplish everything he or she wanted the reader to know?

After you have completed a reading, do a quick analysis of the author's purpose and how well you think he or she executed it by asking yourself these questions:

1. Was the author's purpose for writing the text as clear at the end of the text as it was at the beginning?

2. If it wasn't, where do you think things got off track or where did it change?

3. What do you think the author could have done to maintain the purpose, or do you think the author intended for the purpose to change?

Note that for excerpts like the one in Unit 4, you cannot use the same questions.

Practice Activity: Deciding If the Author's Purpose Was Accomplished

Answer these questions about your experience with Reading 1.

1. Was the author's purpose for writing the text as clear at the end of the text as it was at the beginning?

   _____

   _____

   _____

2. If it wasn't, where do you think things got off track or where did it change?

   _____

   _____

   _____

3. What do you think the author could have done to maintain purpose, or do you think the author intended for the purpose to change?

   _____

   _____

   _____

Practice Activity: Reading for the Big Picture

Put a check mark (✓) next to the statement that best reflects the main idea.

1. _____ It was determined that Pluto is more like a comet than it is like a planet because its body consists of rock and ice.

2. _____ Not everyone agrees with scientists who have concluded that Pluto should no longer be considered a planet.

3. _____ Pluto was officially considered a planet, even after doubts arose, until the word "planet" was officially defined by the IAU in 2006.

Paraphrasing to Simplify

Write a paraphrase that expresses the main points of the original without re-using too many words or phrases from the original.

1. The IAU now considers Pluto and at least 44 other objects, including Charon and Eris, minor or dwarf planets, and minor planets and "regular" planets are too very distinct categories to the IAU.

   _____

   _____

   _____

2. It dominates its "neighborhood" in space by pulling smaller objects either into it or around it as moons.

   _____

   _____

   _____

3. Astronomers knew very little about Pluto. They guessed it was very large and heavy enough to affect Uranus's orbit and that it appeared to be round. These characteristics qualified it to be a planet. However, as space observation became more exact in the 20th century, doubts began to surface.

   _____

   _____

   _____

Writing Strategy: Making an Argument

Academic writers sometimes need to present an argument or persuade the readers to take one side or another on a controversial topic. The writer states an opinion and gives evidence to support why the reader should accept the writer's idea. Writers may write argumentative essays in papers or on exams.

An argumentative piece of writing may not only include the evidence supporting the writer's point of view (state why it is good evidence) but can also discuss evidence for the opposite argument and refute it (explain why it is not good evidence).

Reading 1 contains several sentences that could be used in an essay persuading readers that Pluto should not be a planet.

> *Astronomers knew very little about Pluto. They guessed that it was large and heavy enough to affect Uranus's orbit and it appeared round.* These characteristics qualified it to be a planet. However, as space observation became more exact in the late 20th century, doubts surfaced. *Pluto's largest moon, Charon, was discovered in 1978, and its movements showed Pluto to be much smaller than anyone thought.*

It mentions the opposite side (it was a planet because *it was large and heavy*), but then refutes that statement with a piece of evidence (*Charon showed Pluto to be much smaller*).

An argumentative essay will likely contain several components:

1. a description of the general topic (explaining why there is something to argue about)

2. a sentence that clearly gives the writer's opinion or stance on the topic

3. a summary of the "other" side of the argument

4. reasons why each of those reasons is "wrong"

5. a summary of evidence supporting the writer's opinion

6. reasons why each of those reasons is "right"

7. a conclusion that asks readers to accept the writer's opinion or persuade them to think about it

It is good to use transition words or phrases to show opposite or contrasting ideas:

> *although, but, even though, however, in contrast, nevertheless, on the other hand, though, whereas, while, yet*

Knowing how to present and support your opinion as well as present and refute the opposite view is very helpful in academic studies.

Practice Activity: Making an Argument

Read each of the statements, and then form your own opinion about each one. Write a sentence that includes your opinion, the opposite view, and a reason why the opposing view should be refuted. The first one has been done for you as an example.

1. Pluto's status as a planet

    I don't believe Pluto should be considered a planet. Although it orbits the sun, it never pulled smaller objects into it or around it as moons.

2. military service requirements for all men when they turn 18

    _____

    _____

    _____

3. second language study requirements for college students

    _____

    _____

    _____

4. abolishing team sports

    _____

    _____

    _____

5. the top priority for world leaders

    _____

    _____

    _____

6. working for a small company instead of a large company

    _____

    _____

    _____

Short Writing Tasks

Write a response to each task following the directions given for length and source material.

Task 1 (Summary)

> Look again at Reading 1. Write a one-paragraph summary of the reading. Do not simply copy from the reading. A suggested approach is to make a list of key words and main ideas from the reading and then to not look at the reading again. Review the box on page 15. Use only your notes as you prepare your own summary. Be sure to mention or cite your source. (Length: 5–7 sentences)

_____

_____

_____

_____

_____

_____

_____

Task 2 (Research)

> Write an argumentative paragraph supporting the opinion that Pluto should be a planet. Use information from the reading, and do some light research to find evidence. State your opinion, offer the opposing view using information from the reading, and then refute it using evidence from your own sources before giving the reason for your opinion. Take notes in the space provided. Then write your paragraph on a separate piece of paper. (Length: 5–7 sentences)

_____

_____

_____

_____

_____

_____

Part 2: The Hubble Telescope

Getting Started

You have probably heard of the Hubble Telescope or have seen photographs taken from the telescope. These photographs appear so often in newspapers, magazines, science books and journals, and online sources that we almost take them for granted. Yet the Hubble Telescope is an amazing piece of equipment. It is dependent on inter-connections with other pieces of very advanced technology and on the people who maintain the telescope and monitor, analyze, and interpret the data it sends back. Answer these questions with a partner.

1. Have you ever owned a telescope? If so, what did you look at?

   _____

   _____

   _____

   _____

2. Have you ever been in an area without artificial light at night and seen the sky full of stars? If so, where were you? Did you try to identify specific stars or constellations?

   _____

   _____

   _____

   _____

3. Have you ever visited an observatory or a planetarium? If so, describe the experience. What did you like about it?

   _____

   _____

   _____

   _____

   Reading 2, from a reference book, gives a brief history of the development of the Hubble Space Telescope and then describes how it works.

Before reading an academic passage word for word, it is a good idea to scan for specific information. Scanning will familiarize you with the content, help you notice key information, and improve your comprehension.

Before Reading Strategy: Scanning for Specific Information

Some academic reading contains a lot of statistics or important data. Often those statistics and data are more important than the other information in the reading or may be the information you need for a test or research paper. In those academic situations, it will be important to know how to scan for specific types of information.

When reading to search, you **scan** quickly over the reading material ONLY to find exactly what you are looking for. Think about when you are looking up a word in a print dictionary, for example. You move your eyes quickly downward to find the word you want. The same is true when scanning a text for information, except you will have to move your eyes both horizontally and vertically.

Don't confuse **scanning** with **skimming** (see Unit 1). Scanning focuses only on specific information. Specific information may include names, dates, or numbers.

For Reading 2 on the Hubble Telescope, you will need to read the passage in full, but for the practice activity, you will have a chance to scan just for specific information.

Practice Activity: Scanning for Specific Information

Answer these questions as you scan Reading 2.

1. In which year did Congress approve the funds for the Hubble Telescope? _____

2. The Hubble Space Telescope was part of which mission into space? _____

3. What type of telescope is Hubble? _____

4. The two types of mirrors are what types and sizes?

   (1) _____

   (2) _____

5. How many computers help Hubble operate? _____

6. How often does Hubble circle the Earth? _____

During Reading Strategy: Using Signal Words to Provide Clues to Understanding

You will encounter some useful transition signals when you read texts that explain a process or how something works, as Reading 2 does.

Some of the most common signal words and phrases are related to **sequence** or numbers like *first, second, third*. Similar to these are phrases such as, *after that, next, before, earlier than, prior to, following, then, subsequently,* or *finally*.

Reading 2 uses dates and other time phrases:

In 1946 . . .

After a long delay due to the Challenger disaster . . .

The phrases help give readers a better understanding of the text. These types of clues can be very useful in academic reading, especially when you are reading something outside your subject area or new or challenging information.

Other signal words indicate **similarity** (*likewise, in addition to, in the same way*) or **contrast** (*however, on the other hand, although*). These words are used to highlight important relationships between information in the text.

Practice Activity: Identifying Signal Words

Re-read the text to identify the different signal words, and then list them. Try to determine what they are telling readers about what is happening in the text.

1. How many time or sequence signal words or phrases do you find in Paragraphs 1–5? What clues to understanding do they provide?

_____

_____

2. How many similarity signal words or phrases do you find in Paragraphs 6–17? What clues to understanding do they provide?

_____

_____

Vocabulary Power

There are a number of terms and phrases in the reading that you may encounter in other academic settings. Add at least five vocabulary items to your vocabulary notebook or log.

Match the words in bold from the reading on the left with a definition on the right.

1. _____ But this was an **outrageous** idea, considering no one had even launched a rocket into outer space yet.

2. _____ . . . NASA began drafting the **initial** plans for it. . .

3. _____ As the U.S. space program **matured** in the 1960s and 1970s, Spitzer lobbied NASA and Congress to develop a space telescope.

4. _____ The famous telescope was named after U.S. astronomer Edwin Hubble, whose observations of **variable** stars in distant galaxies confirmed that the universe was expanding and gave support to the Big Bang theory.

5. _____ As you might have guessed, these aren't just **ordinary** mirrors that you might gaze in to admire your reflection.

6. _____ When the HST is in the Earth's shadow, energy that has been stored in onboard batteries can **sustain** the telescope for 7.5 hours.

7. _____ Two of the three sensors find guide stars around the target within their **respective** fields of view.

8. _____ . . .with scientists writing thousands of papers based on the telescope's clear-eyed findings on important stuff like the age of the universe, **gigantic** black holes or what stars look like in the throes of death.

a. developed, grew older

b. keep, hold, maintain

c. changing

d. large in size

e. average, normal

f. crazy, unbelievable

g. individual, separate

h. beginning, first

Reading

Now, read the passage. Use the signal words and phrases to help you understand as you read.

The Hubble Telescope: How It Works

(1) Have you ever stared at the night sky and wondered what the universe looks like up close? Most of us are forced to stargaze with just our eyes, searching for pinpricks of light in the vast black night. Even if you're lucky enough to have access to a ground-based telescope, whose clarity depends on atmospheric factors such as clouds and weather, it still doesn't offer the kind of lucidity these stunning celestial* objects deserve.

celestial: related to the sky

(2) In 1946, an astrophysicist named Dr. Lyman Spitzer, Jr., proposed that a telescope in space would reveal much clearer images of distant objects than any ground-based telescope. That sounds logical, right? But this was an outrageous idea, considering no one had even launched a rocket into outer space yet.

(3) As the U.S. space program matured in the 1960s and 1970s, Spitzer lobbied NASA and Congress to develop a space telescope. In 1975, the European Space Agency (ESA) and NASA began drafting the initial plans for it, and in 1977, Congress approved the necessary funds. NASA named Lockheed Missiles (now Lockheed Martin) as the contractor that would build the telescope and its supporting systems, as well as assemble and test it.

(4) The famous telescope was named after U.S. astronomer Edwin Hubble, whose observations of variable stars* in distant galaxies confirmed that the universe was expanding and gave support to the Big Bang theory.*

variable stars: stars with an apparent magnitude that changes over time

Big Bang theory: the idea that the universe developed by expanding rapidly from a hot, dense state

(5) After a long delay due to the Challenger disaster in 1986,* the Hubble Space Telescope shot into orbit on April 24, 1990, piggybacking aboard the Discovery space shuttle. Since its launch, Hubble has reshaped our view of space, with scientists writing thousands of papers based on the telescope's clear-eyed findings on important concepts like the age of the universe, gigantic black holes, or what stars look like in the throes of* death.

Challenger disaster: The Space Shuttle Challenger broke apart and fell after take off. Seven crew members were killed.

throes of: spasms or pains of

(6) Like any telescope, the HST has a long tube that is open at one end to let in light. It has mirrors to gather and bring the light to a focus where its "eyes" are located. The HST has several types of "eyes" in the form of various instruments. Just as insects can see ultraviolet light or we humans can see visible light, Hubble must also be able to see the various types of light raining down from the heavens.

(7) Specifically, Hubble is a Cassegrain reflector telescope. That just means that light enters the device through the opening and bounces off the primary mirror to a secondary mirror. The secondary mirror in turn reflects the light through a hole in the center of the primary mirror to a focal point behind the primary mirror. If you drew the path of the incoming light, it would look like the letter "W," except with three downward humps instead of two.

(8) At the focal point, smaller, half-reflective, half-transparent mirrors distribute the incoming light to the various scientific instruments. As you might have guessed, these aren't just ordinary mirrors that you might gaze in to admire your reflection. HST's mirrors are made of glass and coated with layers of pure aluminum (three-millionths of an inch thick) and magnesium fluoride (one-millionth of an inch thick) to make them reflect visible, infrared and ultraviolet light. The primary mirror is 7.9 feet (2.4 meters) in diameter, and the secondary mirror is 1.0 feet (0.3 meters) in diameter.

(9) Hubble isn't only a telescope with highly specialized scientific instruments. It's also a spacecraft. As such, it must have power, communicate with the ground and be able to change its attitude (orientation).

(10) All of the instruments and computers on board the HST require electrical power. Two large solar panels fulfill this responsibility. Each wing-like panel can convert the sun's energy into 2,800 watts of electricity. When the HST is in the Earth's shadow, energy that has been stored in onboard batteries can sustain the telescope for 7.5 hours.

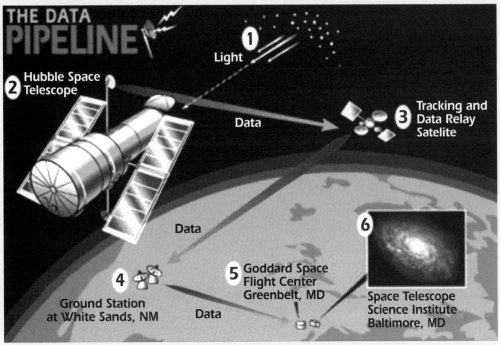

Photo used courtesy of NASA.

(11) In addition to generating power, the HST must be able to talk with controllers on the ground to relay data and receive commands for its next targets. To communicate, the HST uses a series of relay satellites called the Tracking and Data Relay Satellite (TDRS) system. Currently, there are five TDRS satellites in various locations in the sky.

(12) Hubble's communication process is also helped by the two main computers that fit around the telescope's tube above the scientific instrument bays. One computer talks to the ground to transmit data and receive commands. The other computer is responsible for steering the HST and various "housekeeping" functions. Hubble also has backup computers in the event of an emergency.

(13) But what's used to retrieve data? And what happens to that information after it has been collected? Four antennae positioned on the telescope transmit and receive information between Hubble and the Flight Operations Team at the Goddard Space Flight Center in Greenbelt, Md. After receiving the information, Goddard sends it to the Space Telescope Science Institute (STScI) in Maryland, where it's translated into scientific units, such as wavelength or brightness.

(14) Hubble zooms around the Earth every 97 minutes, so focusing on a target can be difficult. Three onboard systems allow the telescope to remain fixed on an object: gyroscopes, the Fine Guidance Sensors, and reaction wheels.

(15) The gyroscopes keep track of Hubble's gross movements. Like compasses, they sense its motion, telling the flight computer that Hubble has moved away from the target. The flight computer then calculates how much and in what direction Hubble must move to remain on target. The flight computer then directs the reaction wheels to move the telescope.

(16) Hubble's fine guidance sensors help keep the telescope fixed on its target by sighting on guide stars. Two of the three sensors find guide stars around the target within their respective fields of view. Once found, they lock onto the guide stars and send information to the flight computer to keep the guide stars within their field of view. The sensors are more sensitive than the gyroscopes, but the combination of gyroscopes and the sensors can keep the HST fixed on a target for hours, despite the telescope's orbital motion.

(17) The HST can't use rocket engines or gas thrusters to steer like most satellites do, because the exhaust gases would hover near the telescope and cloud the surrounding field of view. Instead, the HST has reaction wheels oriented in the three directions of motion (x/y/z or pitch/roll/yaw). The reaction wheels are flywheels, like those found in a clutch.* When the HST needs to move, the flight computer tells one or more flywheels which direction to spin in and how fast, which provides the action force. In accordance with Newton's third law of motion (for every action there is an equal and opposite reaction), the HST spins in the opposite direction of the flywheels until it reaches its target.

clutch: a mechanical machine that allows for power

After Reading Strategy: Evaluating the Reading Experience

When you finish a difficult reading or a reading on a topic that is new to or challenging for you, it's important to reflect on the strategies you employed to understand the reading. Research on what good readers do shows that this step is an important one in improving reading skills because it helps readers understand which strategies work better for them than others, which can lead to more efficient reading overall.

After you have completed a reading, do a quick analysis of the experience by asking yourself these questions:

1. How much of this reading did I understand? 100%, 50%, very little

2. Which parts of the text were the easiest to understand? Why?

3. Which parts of the text were the hardest to understand? Why?

4. Which before, during, or after reading strategies did I use to help me understand the text?

Practice Activity: Evaluating the Reading Experience

Answer these questions about your experience with Reading 2.

1. How much of this reading did I understand?

_____

2. Which parts of the text were the easiest to understand? Why?

_____

_____

3. Which parts of the text were the hardest to understand? Why?

_____

_____

4. Which before, during, or after reading strategies (other than the ones provided in this unit) did you use to help you understand the text?

_____

_____

Practice Activity: Reading for the Big Picture

Put a check mark (✓) next to the statements that best reflect the main ideas.

1. _____ The origins of the Hubble Space Telescope go back to Lyman Spitzer, who suggested that a telescope in space would get clearer pictures than a telescope on the ground.

2. _____ The Discovery space shuttle took the Hubble Space Telescope into space.

3. _____ The Hubble Telescope uses ordinary mirrors to reflect the images that we receive.

4. _____ Hubble is the first telescope to be completely independent of any instruments on the ground.

5. _____ Gyroscopes and sensors are used to keep Hubble fixed on a target for hours even when the telescope is in motion.

Paraphrasing to Simplify

Write a paraphrase that expresses the main points of the original without re-using too many words or phrases from the original.

1. The flight computer then calculates how much and in what direction Hubble must move to remain on target.

   _____

   _____

   _____

   _____

2. The HST can't use rocket engines or gas thrusters to steer like most satellites do, because the exhaust gases would hover near the telescope and cloud the surrounding field of view.

   _____

   _____

   _____

   _____

3. That just means that light enters the device through the opening and bounces off the primary mirror to a secondary mirror.

   _____

   _____

   _____

   _____

Writing Strategy: Writing about a Process

Writing about a process or about how something works is a very common type of academic writing. A good way to organize process writing is using chronological order. You can use chronological order in all types of disciplines. For example, you can explain historical events in History classes, describe a process in Engineering or Science courses, or explain what happened in a story in Literature courses.

When you are describing a process or how something works, you should write about the steps in the order they happen. Depending on the length of your writing, each step should be in its own sentence (in a paragraph) or its own paragraph (in an essay). Make sure your reader understands what you are writing about by using a clear thesis statement:

> There are several steps to follow to properly use a telescope.
>
> The astronomy lab procedure has three steps.

When possible, you can detail the steps in your thesis statement:

> There are three things to do if you want to be an amateur astronomer: choose the proper telescope, research the area of sky you want to view, and arrange a schedule for viewing.

When you write about a process or how something works, it is a good idea to use time signal words and phrases that help your readers follow the content:

> first, second, third
>
> then, next, later
>
> before, during, after
>
> when, while, meanwhile
>
> as, as soon as, since

Organizing chronologically helps keep your essay organized and easy to read. This is very helpful when you have to write essays or describe a process on a test.

Practice Activity: Writing about a Process

Work with a partner. List the steps in each of the processes here and on page 104 on a separate sheet of paper. Decide which steps you would include in your essay. Then write a thesis statement in the space provided that you could use to write a paragraph.

1. how to look for a job

   _____

   _____

2. how to buy a car

   _____

   _____

3. how to study for a science test

   _____

   _____

4. how to have a wedding (in your native culture)

   _____

   _____

5. how to wash clothes

   _____

   _____

6. how a cell phone works

   _____

   _____

7. how a coffee machine works

   _____

   _____

8. how the school's registration process works

   _____

   _____

9. how your favorite game is played

_____

_____

10. how to make a pizza

_____

_____

 ## Your Active Vocabulary in the Real World

Vocabulary is important. Some words are useful for your speaking or for your writing, but other words are useful for your reading or your listening. For each word, decide how you think you will probably need this word for your English. Put a check mark (✓) under the ways you think you are likely to need the word. It is possible to have a check mark in more than one column.

	YOUR VOCABULARY	I need to be able to use this word in WRITING.	I need to be able to use this word in SPEAKING.	I need to understand this word in READING.	I need to understand this word in LISTENING.
1.	assemble				
2.	expanding				
3.	fulfill				
4.	instruments				
5.	matured				
6.	primary				
7.	relay				
8.	secondary				
9.	series				
10.	specialized				

Rapid Vocabulary Review

From the three answers on the right, circle the one that best explains, is an example of, or combines with vocabulary word on the left as it is used in this unit.

Vocabulary	Answers		
Synonyms			
1. primary	first	main	only
2. ordinary	similar	unusual	normal
3. relay (v.)	send	give	receive
4. mature (v.)	grow older	look bigger	smell better
5. initial	first	main	only
6. fund (n.)	money	noise	population
7. expand	no change	more area	outrageous
8. assemble	call off	seem wrong	put together
9. hover	in the air	on land	in the water
10. remove	add	multiply	subtract
11. spin	pair	reach	turn
12. transparent	abnormal	invisible	unlikely
Combinations and Associations			
13. ____ close	over	up	on
14. due ____	under	in	to
15. a ____ of	guilt	multitude	reason
16. ____ than	small	smaller	smallest
17. in a distant ____	delay	function	galaxy
18. a wealthy ____	car	family	product
19. after doubts ____	arose	orbited	searched
20. outer ____	funds	piggybacking	space

⊏╳⊐ Synthesizing: Writing Projects

In-Class Assignments	Outside Assignments
Solar Systems	A Constellation
Some people believe there is life in other solar systems. State your opinion on this topic, summarize opposing viewpoints, and then give examples or evidence to support your claim. **Suggested Length:** 300 words **Preparation:** none	Choose a constellation to describe. Include factual information about the stars and their position in the sky, and also include any mythological information related to the constellation. **Suggested Length:** 800 words **Preparation:** Light research in a library or online
Process Preservation	Celestial Events Interview and Report
Choose something that you do everyday that is a process or an event that is important in your field of study. Describe the steps in the process using signal words and phrases to help someone not familiar with the process to better understand. Prepare a short but detailed presentation for class. **Suggested Length:** 500 words **Preparation:** none	Research popular fears about celestial events online. Look up information related to: • Second sun or nemeses sun or Planet X or Nibiru • Esoteric religions and Sirius • Full Disclosure • Area 51 Choose two of these topics. Then think of six questions to ask about them. Interview two people about their beliefs. Write an essay that summarizes your research. **Suggested Length:** 1,000 words **Preparation:** Research online; personal interviews

Vocabulary Log

To increase your vocabulary knowledge, write a definition or translation for each vocabulary item. Then write an original phrase, sentence, or note that will help you remember the vocabulary item.

Vocabulary Item	Definition or Translation	Your Original Phrase, Sentence, or Note
1. gaze	look at for a long time	He gazed at the stars.
2. secondary		
3. transmit		
4. vast		
5. hover		
6. incoming		
7. lobby		
8. outrageous		
9. variable		
10. retrieve		
11. gross		
12. sustain		
13. sensitive		
14. exhaust		

Vocabulary Item	Definition or Translation	Your Original Phrase, Sentence, or Note
15. target		
16. combination		
17. fixed		
18. calculate		
19. compass		
20. translate		
21. steering		
22. backup (adj.)		
23. panel		
24. orientation		
25. lucidity		

4 Literature: *To Kill a Mockingbird*

Literature is the study of written works—usually fiction and nonfiction. Some of the earliest literary works date back to Babylonian times. Today, literature is studied in universities but appreciated outside the classroom as well. One common type of literature is the novel. Some novels become very well-known and are read by millions of people, even years after they are written. This unit is about one novel that is still popular today.

Part 1: A Famous Novel

Getting Started

Many towns have libraries or historical sites dedicated to writers, artists, actors, and other famous people who were born there. Also, many have celebrations honoring birthdays of famous residents or marking special anniversaries of significant contributions they made. Answer these questions with a partner.

1. Are there any important people from your hometown or the general area where you are from? If so, who are they? Why are they important?

   _____

   _____

   _____

2. Have you ever attended an event in honor of a famous person? If so, who? If living, was the person in attendance? What was the event like?

   _____

   _____

   _____

3. Why do towns spend money hosting events connected with important residents? What are some other ways that significant cultural contributions are honored or celebrated today?

   _____

   _____

   _____

Reading 1 is from a special report about the 50th anniversary of a famous American novel called *To Kill a Mockingbird*. This reading discusses the widespread and lasting fame—and critical acclaim—of the novel written by Harper Lee of Monroeville, Alabama. It reports on celebrations planned to mark the novel's anniversary and the author's avoidance of the spotlight.

To be a successful academic reader, you can use the SQ3R strategy: **Survey, Question, Read, Recite,** and **Review.**

Before Reading Strategy: Using SQ3R—Survey and Question

The SQ3R reading strategy is designed to help you read effectively so you can improve comprehension, write stronger papers, and perform better on tests about texts you have read. The first two letters in the SQ3R reading strategy stand for Survey and Question, and they should be done before you read.

Survey

Surveying helps you develop a broad overview of the reading. There are several parts of the reading you should survey before you read in-depth. By noticing these parts, you are recognizing important features and can form questions about the content.

- title
- headings and subheadings
- review questions
- objectives
- first paragraph
- last paragraph
- summary

Question

After you have completed a survey, you should focus on questions, those you write yourself and those provided by the author or your instructor.

- Convert the title, headings, and subheadings into questions.
- Read any review questions provided in the text or by your instructor.
- Create questions from the objectives given in the book.
- Think about questions that come to mind after you skimmed the first and last paragraphs.
- Ask yourself questions about what the instructor wants you to learn.
- Ask yourself what you already know about the topic.
- Ask yourself questions about what you hope to learn.

Leave room in your notebook for annotations to answer the questions later. Completing the survey and question steps before you read will strengthen your comprehension. It will also help you prepare for future readings. For example, in literature, you may read about a novel and then be assigned to read the actual novel.

Practice Activity: Using SQ3R—Survey and Question

Survey Reading 1, and then develop questions. Then answer the three questions given. A question from the title has been done for you as an example.

Title: _Why is To Kill a Mockingbird still endearing after 50 years?_

Heading 1: _____

Heading 2: _____

Question from Introductory Paragraph: _____

Question from Concluding Paragraph: _____

What do I know about this topic? _____

What do I want to learn about this topic? _____

Why does the instructor want me to read this? _____

During Reading Strategy: Using SQ3R—Read

The third letter in the SQ3R reading strategy stands for the first of the 3Rs. The first R stands for Read. Read does not mean that you will simply read the text passively. Instead, you will read actively. There are several things you should do as you are reading the text.

1. Look for answers to the questions you raised during the Survey and Question phases of the strategy. Write notes in the space you left by the questions or annotate the reading when you find the answers.

2. Answer the questions you created from the title, headings, and sub-headings.

3. Notice pictures, charts, graphs, or other illustrations, and read the captions.

4. Read slowly when there is new or challenging information.

5. Read carefully when you see words or phrases in bold or italic print or those called out in the margins. Make a list of new words or phrases, and add those to your vocabulary log.

A careful, thorough reading will not only help you understand the main idea and details, but will also help you concentrate on vocabulary. Thinking about the information during reading will also help you determine the author's purpose and draw conclusions.

Practice Activity: Using SQ3R—Read

As you read, answer the questions about the introductory and concluding paragraphs you wrote on page 112. Then answer these questions with a partner.

1. Did you find answers to your questions?

   _____

   _____

   _____

2. What vocabulary words or phrases were glossed? What other vocabulary words or phrases did you notice?

   _____

   _____

   _____

3. Were there any pictures? What were they illustrating? Why do you think they were included?

   _____

   _____

   _____

4. Were there any parts of the reading you found challenging and that you slowed your speed for? What were they?

   _____

   _____

   _____

5. Were there any parts of the reading you re-read or wish you had re-read?

   _____

   _____

   _____

Vocabulary Power

There are a number of terms and phrases in this reading that you may encounter in other academic settings. Add at least five vocabulary items to your vocabulary notebook or log.

Match the words in bold from the reading on the left with a definition on the right.

1. _____ July 11, 2010, was the 50th anniversary of the publication of *Mockingbird*, the endearing and **enduring** story of racism and redemption and growing up in a small Southern town during the Depression.

2. _____ . . . *Mockingbird* was made into a film considered as much a **masterpiece** in its medium as the book . . .

3. _____ Not even Oprah could **coax** [Harper Lee] onto her show . . .

4. _____ Especially in Monroeville, where the county courthouse, **featured** in the movie, hosted four days of celebration . . .

5. _____ Teachers and librarians continue to be the book's most **fervent** fans.

6. _____ It **encompasses** multiple themes . . .

7. _____ "It's a great example of literary excellence that is **accessible** to students and highly teachable."

8. _____ "They'd want to know what happens next. That doesn't happen often with **reluctant** readers in high school."

a. understandable; graspable

b. attempt to persuade

c. lasting, continuing, permanent

d. made a focus of, or highlighted

e. enthusiastic, having great feeling for

f. a person's greatest work

g. hesitant; not eager or enthusiastic

h. includes

Reading

Now, read the passage. Use the active reading strategies taught on page 112.

To Kill a Mockingbird:
Endearing, Enduring at 50 Years

By Maria Puente, *USA TODAY*

(1) Thirty-three years after writing *To Kill a Mockingbird*, author Harper Lee, who hadn't been heard from for decades, wrote to her agent, "I am still alive, although very quiet." Today, Lee is still with us and still very quiet, deep in south Alabama. But in the rest of America, it's about to get a whole lot noisier.

(2) July 11, 2010, was the 50th anniversary of the publication of *Mockingbird*, the endearing and enduring story of racism and redemption* and growing up in a small Southern town during the Depression.* It is Lee's only book and one of the handful that could earn the title of Great American Novel.

> **redemption:** to get or win back
>
> **Depression:** the Great Depression, a serious economic downturn in the 1930s in the U.S.

(3) "It's our national novel," proclaims Oprah Winfrey. "It changed how people think," said former first lady and lifetime book lover Laura Bush at a national book festival in 2003. "Best Novel of the Century," according to a poll of librarians by *Library Journal* in 1999. "The one book that millions of us have in common," says Mary McDonagh Murphy, author of a new book of interviews of famous folk talking about how *Mockingbird* changed them, and changed the country. "It has 'book charisma,' a term I rarely use," says Karen MacPherson, children-and-teens librarian at the public library of Takoma Park, Md.

(4) So, not just any old book.

(5) Set in 1930s Maycomb, Ala. (a stand-in for Lee's hometown, Monroeville), it's the story

Gregory Peck, who starred in the movie version, refers to the book while on the movie set.

of upstanding lawyer Atticus Finch, who defends a black man falsely accused of rape in a time and place when that could get a man killed. The story is told through the eyes of Atticus' small tomboy daughter, Scout, and features, among many memorable characters, her neighbor pal Dill, based on Lee's childhood friend, the writer Truman Capote, who spent his early years in Monroeville.

(6) Read by millions, beloved by English teachers and students alike (which is rare), *Mockingbird* was made into a film considered as much a masterpiece in its medium as the book (also rare). There are more than 30 million copies of the book in print, it's never been out of print, nearly 1 million are sold every year, it remains a best seller (it's No. 56 on USA TODAY's Best-Selling Books list), and it's still widely studied in high schools and middle schools across the land.

(7) In celebration of 50 years, Lee's current publisher, HarperCollins, bookstores, libraries and scores of writers and readers across the country are preparing to give Lee and *Mockingbird* a grand shout-out this summer with new editions, new books, readings, stagings and screenings of the 1962 movie.

(8) Miss Nelle Harper Lee (her full name), 84 and slowed by a stroke,* will not be participating—no surprise. She has resolutely refused to play the fame game since about 1964, when, unnerved by the overwhelming public response to the 1960 novel, she went home to Monroeville and closed her door. She had once half-joked that she wanted to be the Jane Austen of south Alabama; now she just wants to be left alone.

> **stroke:** loss of movement, feeling, or awareness caused by a blockage or breaking of a blood vessel in the brain

(9) Not even Oprah could coax her onto her show, although Lee did write a story about learning to read for *O* magazine in 2006. Lee's last major public appearance was in 2007, when she was awarded the Presidential Medal of Freedom at the White House by President Bush; she didn't say much in public then, either.

(10) "Public encouragement," she told a radio interviewer in 1964. "I hoped for a little but I got rather a whole lot, and in some ways this was just about as frightening as the quick, merciful death (of the book) I'd expected." Just imagine how she'd view the contemporary media. "Harper Lee has always been a very private person, and the legacy of her book speaks for itself," says Tina Andreadis, spokeswoman for HarperCollins.

(11) But never mind. Leave her be; everyone will toast her in absentia.

Big Party in Monroeville

(12) Especially in Monroeville, where the county courthouse, featured in the movie, hosted four days of celebration, including a birthday party on the lawn, a marathon reading, silent auctions, a walking tour of the town, and a screening of a new state-funded documentary, *Our Mockingbird*, that examines issues of race, class and injustice through the lens of the book.

(13) It's one of 50 commemorations HarperCollins has helped organize in bookstores and libraries across the country, including: Former NBC anchorman Tom Brokaw will do a reading in a bookstore in Bozeman, Mont. In a Rhinebeck, N.Y., bookstore this weekend, the locals are planning a party featuring trivia, "mocktails" and music on the stereo by the indie band Boo Radleys.

(14) HarperCollins also is publishing four new special anniversary editions, plus Murphy's book, *Scout, Atticus & Boo: A Celebration of Fifty Years of To Kill a Mockingbird*, which features interviews with Oprah; Brokaw; singer Rosanne Cash; Lee's sister, Alice Finch Lee (98 and still working as a lawyer in Monroeville); and even Mary Badham, who at age 10 played Scout in the movie and was nominated for an Oscar.

(15) "You don't (often) get a chance to have a film and a book that makes that kind of impact," Badham tells Murphy. "It's about a way of life, getting along and learning tolerance. This is not a black-and-white 1930s issue. This is a global issue." Murphy, who also has produced a film documentary of the book that will be shown at film festivals this summer, says *Mockingbird* still matters because racial prejudice still exists, even though the first African-American president resides in the White House. "There are very few books where the characters are unforgettable, the story is suspenseful in the best kind of dramatic way, and it has a social message without being preachy," Murphy says.

(16) It encompasses multiple themes: coming of age, tolerance and empathy, fatherhood and hero worship, and the eccentricities of small-town people. It's also about racism and incest, murder and injustice, fear and ignorance, and the possibility of redemption.

(17) "It was meant to be a gift to her father," says Charles Shields, author of *Mockingbird: A Portrait of Harper Lee*. "She wanted to write a love story from a daughter to a father, who was a great man in a small town and the model for Atticus." Like Atticus, A.C. Lee was a lawyer and once defended black men accused of murder.

(18) Teachers and librarians continue to be the book's most fervent fans. "I think about this book at least once a day—it's magic, the way she uses language and the characters she creates, there's a stickiness to them," says Gary Anderson, an English and American studies teacher (30 years) at William Fremd High School in Palatine, Ill., who taught the book for years. "It's a great example of literary excellence that is accessible to students and highly teachable."

A Hit with 'Reluctant Readers'

(19) Best-selling author Wally Lamb (*She's Come Undone*), a former teacher who taught the book for 25 years, says it was rare to encounter students indifferent to the book. "After the first chapter, they would read it voluntarily, read ahead of the assignments," Lamb says. "They'd want to know what happens next. That doesn't happen often with reluctant readers in high school." *Mockingbird* is not without critics. The black characters in the book are the least developed, the most stereotypical, especially the defendant Tom Robinson. James McBride, author of *The Color of Water: A Black Man's Tribute to His White Mother*, says Lee could have handled the Robinson character better, but he still thinks she's an American treasure. "What other writer during that time was willing to take on this subject with the kind of honesty and integrity that she did?" he told Murphy for her book. "What other white writer? I can't think of anyone."

(20) Winfrey positively gushes about the book and Lee, and especially Scout. "You just liked Scout," she told Murphy. "You connected with her. I liked her energy. I liked the spirit of her. I liked the freshness of her. I liked the fact that she was so curious. I loved this character so much."

(21) But Atticus (Gregory Peck won an Oscar playing him in the movie) can come off as "a bit of a plaster saint," says Shields, always reminding Scout that you can't really know someone until you've walked in his shoes.

(22) Although it may read as if it just spooled out of the storyteller, Lee actually struggled with the novel for years in the 1950s while working at menial jobs (airline reservation clerk) in New York. Then some Alabama friends in town gave her a Christmas gift of enough money to quit her job and work full time on the book for a year. A skilled editor helped her turn a series of stories and vignettes* into a seamless whole.

vignettes: short literary works

(23) It was published after she accompanied Capote to Kansas to help him research an infamous murder there that eventually became his best work, *In Cold Blood*. Lee's book won a Pulitzer Prize; Capote's did not, and he was envious, which damaged their friendship. It didn't help that Capote failed to credit her for her contributions to his book, and failed to deny false rumors that *he* was the author of *Mockingbird*.

(24) The question everyone asks to this day: Why did Lee not write another book? Shields says some people believe there is another novel but it won't be published until after her death. Lee's sister Alice continues to insist there will not be another book. At one point, Shields reports, one of her cousins asked Lee when she would produce another book. Nelle's reply: "When you're at the top, there's only one way to go."

After Reading Strategy: Using SQ3R—Recite and Review

The final two Rs in the SQ3R reading strategy stand for Recite and Review. Recite and review are actually done after you finish reading.

Recite

- Ask yourself questions about what you read.

- Summarize the reading in your own words.

- Look at your notes, and read your answers to the questions.

- Say the vocabulary words and phrases, and take time to learn their definitions.

Do these actions aloud so that you are hearing and seeing the material simultaneously. By doing so, you are using two senses (sight and hearing) and are more likely to remember. To further develop the reciting of material, you can write notes.

Review

Don't wait until it is time for a test or time to write a paper to review the reading material.

- After you recite, continue to read your answers to questions, and write new questions and answers in the margins.

- Make sure to answer questions about the main ideas.

- Draw conclusions about the topic.

- Try to recite or write answers from memory.

- Make guesses about any information that may be asked about later.

It helps to create a SQ3R chart or graph (see page 121) to help you organize all the questions and answers during the Review stage. Put your questions in the left column and your answers in the right column. You can then study from this chart each day.

Completing the five parts of the SQ3R reading strategy help you get to know the reading material well. If you do so, you will not have to "cram" for an exam or spend as much time re-reading later.

After Reading Strategy: Completing a SQ3R Chart

Complete the SQ3R chart with your questions and annotations from the reading. Make sure to also include notes about the main ideas, conclusions, and vocabulary.

Questions or Annotations	Answers or Details
Questions from titles and headings:	
Notes about pictures or illustrations:	
Notes about my annotations:	
Questions from the reading:	
Questions from reciting:	
What are the main ideas?	
What conclusions can be drawn?	
What vocabulary items are important?	

Practice Activity: Reading for the Big Picture

Put a check mark (✓) next to the statements that best reflect the main ideas.

1. _____ Oprah Winfrey and librarians loved the character of Scout.

2. _____ *To Kill a Mockingbird* is a novel that has remained popular, loved, and respected for more than 50 years.

3. _____ Harper Lee, the author of the book, never wrote another novel and has tried to avoid public appearances related to her book.

4. _____ In the movie based on the book, Gregory Peck played the character of Atticus Finch, the father of Scout and a lawyer representing a black man accused of rape.

5. _____ Many events were scheduled and held across the nation to celebrate the 50th anniversary of the novel.

Paraphrasing to Simplify

Write a paraphrase that expresses the main points of the original without re-using too many words or phrases from the original.

1. July 11, 2010, was the 50th anniversary of the publication of *Mockingbird*, the endearing and enduring story of racism and redemption and growing up in a small Southern town during the Depression.

   _____

   _____

   _____

2. She has resolutely refused to play the fame game since about 1964, when, unnerved by the overwhelming public response to the 1960 novel, she went home to Monroeville and closed her door.

   _____

   _____

   _____

3. It didn't help that Capote failed to credit her for her contributions to his book, and fialed to deny false rumors that *he* was the author of *Mockingbird*.

   _____

   _____

   _____

Writing Strategy: Using Facts as Support

When writing an academic paper, you sometimes have to include support statements about the topic. One way to do this is to give facts. To do so, you have to be able to distinguish between facts and opinions. Facts are objective statements that can be supported with proof from another source. Opinions are subjective and are usually based on someone's attitude or belief.

Opinion: *To Kill a Mockingbird* is one of the best novels ever written.

Fact: *To Kill a Mockingbird* is one of the best-selling novels ever written.

Although you can offer opinions in academic writing, they can't be used as support. Facts, however, can be used.

Even facts, however, sometimes need proof or additional details. By adding additional details, your facts can be even stronger. The example about Lee's book being a best-selling novel is actually a fact that needs proof or details.

According to *USA Today, To Kill a Mockingbird* has sold more than 30 million copies and sells almost a million copies every year.

Facts can be contradictory. Make sure to state when certain information is disputed by others.

- Be as specific as possible.
- Use sources that are less than five years old if possible.
- Credit the source.
- Distinguish fact from opinion for your reader.

Practice Activity: Distinguishing Fact from Opinion

Read the quotations from and statements based on information from the first part of Reading 1 (pages 115–16). Decide whether each one is a fact or an opinion.

1. _____ "It's our national novel."

2. _____ Not even Oprah could coax [Harper Lee] onto her show, although Lee did write a story about learning to read for *O Magazine* in 2006.

3. _____ "It has 'book charisma,' a term I rarely use."

4. _____ There are more than 30 million copies of the book in print, it's never been out of print, nearly 1 million are sold every year, it remains a best seller. . . .

5. _____ It's no surprise that that Miss Nelle Harper Lee won't participate in the celebration.

6. _____ Miss Lee would not like the contemporary media.

7. _____ "Public encouragement, I hoped for a little but I got rather a whole lot. . . ."

8. _____ The book was made into a film considered as much a masterpiece in its medium as the book itself.

9. _____ It remains a best seller; it's number *56* on *USA Today's* Best-Selling Books list.

10. _____ It's still widely studied in high schools and middle schools across the land.

Compare your answers with a partner. Which are facts and which of those facts can use more proof or details? How can you make that happen? How could the opinions be converted into facts?

Then, read the second part of Reading 1 (pages 117–18) again. Highlight the facts in one color and the opinions in a second color. Talk about your highlighted statements with a partner.

Short Writing Tasks

Write a response to each task following the directions given for length and source material.

Task 1 (Summary)

Look again at Reading 1. Write a one-paragraph summary of the reading. Do not simply copy from the reading. A suggested approach is to make a list of key words and main ideas from the reading and then to not look at the reading again. Review the box on page 15. Use only your notes as you prepare your own summary. Be sure to mention or cite your source. (Length: 5–7 sentences)

_____

_____

_____

_____

_____

_____

_____

Task 2 (Research)

Reading 1 discusses a novel and the impact it has had on readers. Based on your instuctor's guidelines, do some light research online or in a library to find information about another American book or movie that has been popular for many years. It can be for children, teenagers, or adults. Name and describe the book or movie, identify the author, and tell why the book has been popular. Be sure to list your source information. Take notes in the space provided. Then write your paragraph on a separate piece of paper. (Length: 8–12 sentences)

_____

_____

_____

_____

_____

_____

Part 2: *To Kill A Mockingbird* by Harper Lee

Getting Started

Reading novels is a hobby for many people. Even people who do not enjoy reading all the time have a favorite novel or book that they remember. Answer these questions with a partner.

1. What is your favorite novel or the book you most remember? What is the story about?

   _____

   _____

   _____

   _____

2. What is it that you like about your favorite novel? When did you first read it? Have you read it more than once? Do you think you will read it again?

   _____

   _____

   _____

   _____

3. Think about your relationship with a parent or another important older relative or mentor. Has your view of this person changed since you were a child? Do you think you understand this person well now?

   _____

   _____

   _____

   _____

Reading 2 is an excerpt from *To Kill a Mockingbird*, Harper Lee's book that was the subject of Reading 1. As you learned, the story is told from the point of view of a young girl, Scout. Her father, Atticus Finch, is a lawyer. Atticus is defending Tom Robinson, an African-American man accused of rape. The story takes place during the Depression (the 1930s) in the South—a time and place in which racial injustice was the accepted norm and so the accusation of a serious crime like this could easily mean death for an African-American man.

A typical academic assignment might require you to read an excerpt from a famous piece of literature or important essay. Anthologies (volumes that compile famous texts from certain historical periods) are commonly used textbooks in Literature courses. Anthologies try to provide some context for each reading, but you will need to develop your own strategies for understanding excerpts as well.

Before Reading Strategy: Understanding the Context of an Excerpt

Reading an excerpt from a literary work can be difficult—you don't have the benefit of knowing what happened in the pages before the excerpt, so you have to be prepared to "jump into" the middle of a story. The first thing to do is to determine if you know anything about the book the excerpt is from, such as the information presented in Reading 1 about the novel *To Kill a Mockingbird*. You can also try to activate your own knowledge or get information from your teacher or an online source.

Most excerpts in textbooks or anthologies will be preceded by a short explanation of the excerpt—what part of the novel or work you will be reading and also why the excerpt has been chosen for you to read. In other words, most excerpts will be from important parts of the novel. In addition, there is usually a summary or short synopsis of the work as a whole and its importance before the excerpt too. If no summary of the work as a whole is provided, then you should go to your teacher or search online to try to learn more about the novel or text as a whole. It is very important to have a good idea about the "whole" before you start reading a "piece."

Here is some information about the excerpt you will read:

This excerpt is one in which the narrator, Scout, describes her impressions of her father, Atticus Finch. She describes a conversation she had with her teacher about him. This conversation is the beginning of Scout being able to see how other people in the town see her father in a different way than she does, which is an important theme in this novel.

Practice Activity: Understanding the Context of an Excerpt

Before you begin reading the excerpt from *To Kill a Mockingbird,* review what you know about the novel from Reading 1 and incorporate other knowledge you have.

1. What do you know about the narrator? _____

   _____

   _____

2. About how old is she? _____

3. What is Atticus Finch's profession? _____

4. Who is Jem? _____

5. When and where does this story take place? _____

   _____

6. What do you already know about the story? _____

   _____

   _____

During Reading Strategy: Understanding Point of View

Point of view is important to understanding a novel or text as a whole. If you understand why the narrator or character is saying what he or she is saying, then you will be more successful in understanding the point of the excerpt and more about the story.

Some things you need to think about when considering point of view are:

- Who is the narrator? Is the narrator a character or *omniscient* (one who can see all things happening to all characters)?

- How would the story be different if someone else were telling the story?

- Why do you think one character tells us about a conversation with another character?

- Do you have a better understanding of any of the characters because of this excerpt?

Think about these questions as you read an excerpt.

Practice Activity: Understanding Point of View

Although Scout is the narrator, the points of view of other characters are given in the excerpt. What do we learn in the excerpt about each character listed and what he or she thinks?

1. Scout _____

   _____

2. Jem _____

   _____

3. Atticus _____

   _____

4. Miss Maudie _____

   _____

Vocabulary Power

There are a number of terms and phrases in this excerpt that you may encounter in other academic settings. Add at least five vocabulary items to your vocabulary notebook or log.

Match the words in bold from the reading on the left with a definition on the right.

1. _____ He was much older than the parents of our school **contemporaries**. . . .

2. _____ He was nearly blind in his left eye, and said left eyes were the tribal **curse** of the Finches.

3. _____ With these attributes, however, he would not remain as **inconspicuous** as we wished him to: that year, the school buzzed with talk about him defending Tom Robinson, none of which was complimentary.

4. _____ With these attributes, however, he would not remain as inconspicuous as we wished him to: that year, the school buzzed with talk about him defending Tom Robinson, none of which was **complimentary**.

5. _____ After my bout with Cecil Jacobs when I **committed** myself to a policy of cowardice.

6. _____ After my bout with Cecil Jacobs when I committed myself to a policy of **cowardice**. . . .

7. _____ Shoot all the bluejays you want, if you can hit 'em, but remember it's a **sin** to kill a mockingbird.

8. _____ This modest **accomplishment** served to make me even more ashamed of him.

a. an achievement, something that has been done

b. to make a promise, to become responsible or obligated to something

c. people of the same age or living during the same time

d. having no courage

e. a wish that something harmful happens to someone else

f. not noticeable

g. something evil

h. favorable

Reading

Now, read the passage. Consider the points of view of the different characters as you read.

To Kill a Mockingbird by Harper Lee

Atticus was feeble: he was nearly fifty. When Jem and I asked him why he was so old, he said he got started late, which we felt reflected upon his abilities and manliness. He was much older than the parents of our school contemporaries, and there was nothing Jem or I could say about him when our classmates said, "*My* father—"

Jem was football crazy. Atticus was never too tired to play keep-away, but when Jem wanted to tackle him Atticus would say, "I'm too old for that, son."

Our father didn't do anything. He worked in an office, not in a drugstore. Atticus did not drive a dump-truck for the county, he was not the sheriff, he did not farm, work in a garage, or do anything that could possibly arouse the admiration of anyone.

Besides that, he wore glasses. He was nearly blind in his left eye, and said left eyes were the tribal curse of the Finches. Whenever he wanted to see something well, he turned his head and looked from his right eye.

He did not do the things our schoolmates' fathers did: he never went hunting, he did not play poker or fish or drink or smoke. He sat in the livingroom and read.

With these attributes, however, he would not remain as inconspicuous as we wished him to: that year, the school buzzed with talk about him defending Tom Robinson, none of which was complimentary. After my bout with Cecil Jacobs when I committed myself to a policy of cowardice, word got around that Scout Finch wouldn't fight any more, her daddy wouldn't let her. This was not entirely correct: I wouldn't fight publicly for Atticus, but the family was private ground. I would fight anyone from a third cousin upwards tooth and nail. Francis Hancock, for example, knew that.

When he gave us our air-rifles Atticus wouldn't teach us to shoot. Uncle Jack instructed us in the rudiments thereof; he said Atticus wasn't interested in guns. Atticus said to Jem one day, "I'd rather you shot at tin cans in the back yard, but I know you'll go after birds. Shoot all the bluejays you want, if you can hit 'em, but remember it's a sin to kill a mockingbird."

The famous courtroom scene from the book and movie.

That was the only time I ever heard Atticus say it was a sin to do something, and I asked Miss Maudie about it.

"Your father's right," she said. "Mockingbirds don't do one thing but make music for us to enjoy. They don't eat up people's gardens, don't nest in corncribs, they don't do one thing but sing their hearts out for us. That's why it's a sin to kill a mockingbird."

"Miss Maudie, this is an old neighborhood, ain't it?"

"Been here longer than this town."

"Nome, I mean the folks on our street are all old. Jem and me's the only children around here. Mrs. Dubose is close on to a hundred and Miss Rachel's old and so are you and Atticus."

"I don't call fifty very old," said Miss Maudie tartly. "Not being wheeled around yet, am I? Neither's your father. But I must say Providence was kind enough to burn down that old mausoleum of mine, I'm too old to keep it up—maybe you're right, Jean Louise, this is a settled neighborhood. You've never been around young folks much, have you?"

"Yessum, at school."

"I mean young grown-ups. You're lucky, you know. You and Jem have the benefit of your father's age. If your father was thirty you'd find life quite different."

"I sure would. Atticus can't do anything. . . . "

"You'd be surprised," said Miss Maudie. "There's life in him yet."

"What can he do?"

"Well, he can make somebody's will so airtight can't anybody meddle with it."

"Shoot . . . "

"Well, did you know he's the best checker-player in this town? Why, down at the Landing when we were coming up, Atticus Finch could beat everybody on both sides of the river."

"Good Lord, Miss Maudie, Jem and me beat him all the time."

"It's about time you found out it's because he lets you. Did you know he can play a Jew's Harp*?"

This modest accomplishment served to make me even more ashamed of him.

"*Well* . . . " she said.

"Well, what, Miss Maudie?"

"Well nothing. Nothing—it seems with all that you'd be proud of him.

Jew's Harp: one of the oldest musical instruments in the world, dating back to Asia (there is no connection to Judaism)

After Reading Strategy: Getting a Sense of the Whole

After you read an excerpt, you need to make sure you have an understanding of the whole piece. Just as you needed to get some information about the novel or text before you read, you also need to do this after you read an excerpt.

Getting a sense of the whole broadens your view and helps you understand more than the plot. It helps you draw conclusions about the characters and sense the author's purpose for writing. This strategy will help you begin to analyze the genre, themes, and characters. In general, it improves your comprehension and gives you something to think about and write about later.

In some courses, you may be assigned to read another excerpt from the same book, another reading by the same author, or a text in the same genre.

Practice Activity: Getting a Sense of the Whole

Discuss these questions with a partner.

1. What do you now want to know about the novel *To Kill a Mockingbird* after reading this excerpt? _____

   _____

2. How can you learn the information? _____

   _____

3. What sense of the whole do you share with you partner? Are there any differences? _____

   _____

Practice Activity: Reading for the Big Picture

Write T if the statement is true or F if the statement is false.

1. _____ Scout is ashamed of her father.

2. _____ Jem hates football.

3. _____ Atticus says that it is a sin to kill a mockingbird because mockingbirds only sing; they do no harm.

4. _____ Miss Maudie points out negative things about Scout's father.

5. _____ Atticus has talents such as playing checkers and playing a Jew's Harp.

Paraphrasing to Simplify

Write a paraphrase that expresses the main points of the original without re-using too many words or phrases from the original.

1. After my bout with Cecil Jacobs when I committed myself to a policy of cowardice, word got around that Scout Finch wouldn't fight anymore, her daddy wouldn't let her.

   _____

   _____

   _____

2. You're lucky, you know. You and Jem have the benefit of your father's age. If your father was thirty, you'd find life quite different.

   _____

   _____

   _____

3. Atticus said to Jem one day, "I'd rather you shot at tin cans in the back yard, but I know you'll go after birds. Shoot all the bluejays you want, if you can hit 'em, but remember it's a sin to kill a mockingbird."

   _____

   _____

   _____

Writing Strategy: Preparing a Reader Response

A reader response is a common type of academic writing used in many disciplines. A reader response allows you to write about your personal feelings and ideas about what you've read from your own point of view. But you need to support your ideas with evidence.

A reader response has several characteristics. First, ask yourself questions before beginning to write:

- How does this passage relate to my life?

- Do I agree or disagree with the character or author?

- What did I learn from reading this passage?

- What is my opinion of the theme, character, or events in the passage?

- How do I think this will change my views?

Second, write in the first person. In other words, you will use *I* or *my* in your paper. Give your opinion.

> My opinion is . . .

> I think that . . .

Next, you can use facts from the reading or events from your own life as evidence to support your opinion. Refer to specific details or events in the reading.

> I think the novel was interesting to read because . . .

> I understand why the character said . . .

> I would have done the same thing because . . .

> It reminds me of a situation that happened to me a few years ago . . .

Last, summarize your ideas in a concluding sentence or paragraph.

> In summary, . . .

> In conclusion, . . .

Practice Activity: Writing Responses

Look at this list of research paper topics, and write a statement expressing your opinion. Support your opinion with something you've read, heard, or know about.

1. human behavior

   _____

   _____

2. Ancient Greece

   _____

   _____

3. Pluto

   _____

   _____

4. The world's economy

   _____

   _____

5. your dream job

   _____

   _____

6. the world's biggest problem

   _____

   _____

7. a great leader

   _____

   _____

8. your favorite novel

   _____

   _____

Your Active Vocabulary in the Real World

Vocabulary is important. Some words are useful for your speaking or for your writing, but other words are useful for your reading or your listening. For each word, decide how you think you will probably need this word for your English. Put a check mark (✓) under the correct ways you think you are likely to need the word. It is possible to have a check mark in more than one column.

	YOUR VOCABULARY	I need to be able to use this word in WRITING.	I need to be able to use this word in SPEAKING.	I need to understand this word in READING.	I need to understand this word in LISTENING.
1.	attributes				
2.	bout				
3.	contemporaries				
4.	curious				
5.	endearing				
6.	impact				
7.	integrity				
8.	modest				
9.	sin				
10.	theme				

Rapid Vocabulary Review

From the three answers on the right, circle the one that best explains, is an example of, or combines with vocabulary word on the left as it is used in this unit.

Vocabulary	Answers		
Synonyms			
1. decade	10 days	10 months	10 years
2. handful	few	large	wide
3. rare	common	unusual	popular
4. scores	small number	mid-sized number	large number
5. resides	lives	moves	owns
6. themes	details	problems	topics
7. highly	marginly	extremely	insignificantly
8. deny	say no	say maybe	say yes
9. thorough	fast	delicious	complete
10. attributes	traits	symbols	eccentricities
11. an excerpt	a narrator	a part	a summary
12. modest	average	popular	usual
Combinations and Associations			
13. be ____ of	interested	proud	reluctant
14. a stand- ____	over	on	in
15. through the ____ of	eyes	nose	ears
16. meddle ____ something	in	under	with
17. a way of ____	life	issue	education
18. be willing ____	by	of	to
19. walk in someone's ____	shoes	clothes	path
20. a menial ____	book	job	storm

⊏╳⊐ Synthesizing: Writing Projects

In-Class Assignments	Outside Assignments
A Character Description	**How Does Scout Feel?**
Write a paragraph that describes a favorite character from a novel or from a movie. Include your opinion about the character, and give some facts about the novel or movie and the character's role. **Suggested Length:** 300 words **Preparation:** none	Write a reader response about Scout's feelings about her father. Give your opinion and support your idea by writing about a parent or mentor. Be specific. **Suggested Length:** 800 words **Preparation:** none
Short Synopsis (Plot Summary)	**Comparing Authors or Writings**
Write a paragraph describing the plot (the story) of a novel that you have read. Think about the main events and the characters' points of view. Describe the ways that you think the story might be different if someone else were telling the story. Be specific. Then make a short presentation. **Suggested Length:** 500 words **Preparation:** none	Write a critical essay comparing two pieces of writing by the same author. Read both pieces and compare and contrast them. Remember to add facts as support. **Suggested Length:** 1,000 words **Preparation:** Light research in a library or online

Vocabulary Log

To increase your vocabulary knowledge, write a definition or translation for each vocabulary item. Then write an original phrase, sentence, or note that will help you remember the vocabulary item.

Vocabulary Item	Definition or Translation	Your Original Phrase, Sentence, or Note
1. curious	wanting to know	I'm curious about Australia.
2. charisma		
3. upstanding		
4. medium (n.)		
5. resolutely		
6. merciful		
7. legacy		
8. editions		
9. impact		
10. integrity		
11. be willing to		
12. tooth and nail		
13. arouse		
14. admiration		

Vocabulary Item	Definition or Translation	Your Original Phrase, Sentence, or Note
15. policy		
16. contributions		
17. deny		
18. eventually		
19. willing to		
20. stereotypical		
21. possibility		
22. memorable		
23. unnerved		
24. grand (adj.)		
25. indifferent		

5 Civil Engineering: Bridges

In order to build, engineers must understand and know how to work with the basic properties of materials and the forces that move them. The first reading examines the main types of bridges and then explains how they are constructed and why they work. The second reading explains Hooke's Law, an important concept in physics that engineers use to understand materials and how to work with them.

Part 1: How Bridges Work

Getting Started

Bridges are so common that most people probably don't stop to think about them and how they were designed and built. However, it is because they are so common that they have such a big impact in the world. Answer these questions with a partner.

1. Think of one bridge located near you and one world-famous bridge. Can you describe them?

   _____

   _____

   _____

   _____

2. What are some reasons that people build bridges?

   _____

   _____

   _____

   _____

3. What do you think engineers take into consideration when they design and build a bridge?

   _____

   _____

   _____

   _____

Reading 1 is from a reference book and describes three main types of bridges and their basic design principles.

Like reference books, academic textbooks are designed to introduce students to common and essential topics in a particular field of study. When these topics are written about in academic texts, readers will notice that there is likely a specific text pattern being used by the author.

Before Reading Strategy: Previewing for Text Patterns

When you are assigned a reading about a topic that is new to you or that you know has a lot of technical information in it, one strategy for preparing for the reading is to look for patterns in the structure of the text. Patterns help you get a sense of the material before you start reading and help you determine the author's main ideas. It also makes it easier to follow the reading.

A good first step is to read the subheadings. Then read any material that stands out, like text in lists or text that is in **boldface** or *italic* type. Look for words that indicate a pattern, like numbers—for example, the line in Reading 1 that says *There are three major types of bridges.* This is a good indication that there will be three main sections to the reading.

Other phrasing that might give you information about the reading would be language to indicate the text is going to compare and contrast different items, such as *compared to, in contrast to,* or *a comparison of.*

A cause-and-effect text might include phrases such as *as a result of* or *a consequence of.*

A process or chronological text might include words like *first, then, next, after, when,* or *last.*

Transition words or phrases like *however* and *therefore* are also useful in showing relationships between and among ideas.

Practice Activity: Previewing for Text Patterns

1. Look at Reading 1 on pages 149–54. Read the subheadings. List them.

   _____   _____

   _____   _____

   _____

   How has the author organized the text?

   _____

2. You know from the strategy box on page 145 that the reading will discuss three types of bridges. The subheadings and the first bulleted list reinforce this. Look for phrasing and transitions that indicate what the author is going to write about the three types.

   Are the different types of bridges going to be compared and/or contrasted? What language is used to tell you that (give words and paragraph number)?

   _____

   _____

   _____

3. What does the second bulleted list indicate will also be discussed in the reading?

   _____

   _____

4. Skim Reading 1. How many other times do you find the concepts from the second bulleted list discussed in the reading?

   _____

   _____

During Reading Strategy: Making Text-to-Self Connections

One way that good readers engage with the text is to develop a sort of internal conversation with themselves as they read. They look for ways to make personal connections with the text and its language and concepts to help improve their understanding. Common personal connection questions readers ask or think about are:

> What does this remind me of? This reminds me of. . . .
>
> This is similar to X that I read in X.
>
> This looks like something I once saw in X.
>
> This is confusing to me because of what I read/saw in X.
>
> I agree/disagree with this.
>
> Why would this be true?

Readers think about these types of things as they encounter new information, and as they continue to read, they may change their comment or question or may make new connections. Answers to the questions can also help prepare you for an exam or to write a research paper later.

As you read "How Bridges Work" on pages 149–54, stop when you see each stop sign in the margin, and then answer the corresponding questions on page 155.

Vocabulary Power

There are a number of terms and phrases in this reading that you may encounter in other academic settings. Add at least five vocabulary items to your vocabulary notebook or log.

Match the words in bold from the reading on the left with a definition on the right.

1. _____ A suspension bridge, the pinnacle of bridge technology, is **capable** of spanning up to 7,000 feet (2,100 m).

2. _____ The natural curve of the **arch** and its ability to dissipate the force outward greatly reduces the effects of tension on the underside of the arch.

3. _____ A beam bridge is basically a rigid **horizontal** structure that is resting on two piers, or supports, one at each end.

4. _____ Many beam bridges that you find on highway **overpasses** use concrete or steel beams to handle the load.

5. _____ Many beam bridges that you find on highway overpasses use **concrete** or steel beams to handle the load.

6. _____ Despite the **ingenious** addition of a truss, the beam bridge is still limited in the distance it can span.

7. _____ The center of the beam is made up of the **diagonal** members of the truss, while the top and bottom of the truss represent the top and bottom of the beam.

8. _____ The tension in an arch is **negligible**.

a. level; parallel to the ground

b. insignificant; too small to be important

c. having the ability

d. a hard material made from cement, sand, gravel, and water

e. clever, inventive

f. two lines connecting opposite corners of a square

g. bridge or walkway that goes over a road, railway line, river, etc.

h. curved shape in a doorway or opening that supports the weight above it

Reading

Now, read the passage. Stop at each stop sign, and answer the questions on page 155 as you read.

How Bridges Work

(1) There's no doubt you've seen a bridge, and it's almost as likely that you've traveled over one. If you've ever laid a plank or log down over a stream to keep from getting wet, you've even constructed a bridge. Bridges are truly ubiquitous—a natural part of everyday life. A bridge provides passage over some sort of obstacle: a river, a valley, a road, or a set of railroad tracks.

(2) Here we will look at the three major types of bridges so that you can understand how each one works. The type of bridge used depends on various features of the obstacle. The main feature that controls the bridge type is the size of the obstacle. How far is it from one side to the other?

The Basics

(3) There are three major types of bridges:

- The beam bridge
- The arch bridge
- The suspension bridge

(4) The biggest difference between the three is the distances they can cross in a single **span**. A span is the distance between two bridge supports, whether they are columns, towers, or the wall of a canyon. A modern beam bridge, for instance, is likely to span a distance of up to 200 feet (60 meters), while a modern arch can safely span up to 800 or 1,000 feet (240 to 300 m). A suspension bridge, the pinnacle of bridge technology, is capable of spanning up to 7,000 feet (2,100 m).

(5) What allows an arch bridge to span greater distances than a beam bridge, or a suspension bridge to span a distance seven times that of an arch bridge? The answer lies in how each bridge type deals with two important forces called **compression** and **tension**:

- **Compression** is a force that acts to compress or shorten the thing it is acting on.
- **Tension** is a force that acts to expand or lengthen the thing it is acting on.

(6) A simple, everyday example of compression and tension is a spring. When we press down, or push the two ends of the spring together, we compress it. The force of compression shortens the spring. When we pull up, or pull apart the two ends, we create tension in the spring. The force of tension lengthens the spring.

(7) Compression and tension are present in all bridges, and it's the job of the bridge design to handle these forces without buckling or snapping. **Buckling** is what happens when the force of compression overcomes an object's ability to handle compression, and **snapping** is what happens when the force of tension overcomes an object's ability to handle tension. The best way to deal with these forces is to either dissipate them or transfer them. To **dissipate** force is to spread it out over a greater area, so that no one spot has to bear the brunt of the concentrated force. To **transfer** force is to move it from an area of weakness to an area of strength, an area designed to handle the force. An arch bridge is a good example of dissipation, while a suspension bridge is a good example of transference.

The Beam Bridge

(8) A beam bridge is basically a rigid horizontal structure that is resting on two piers, or supports, one at each end. The weight of the bridge and any traffic on it is directly supported by the piers. The weight is traveling directly downward.

(9) The force of compression manifests itself on the top side of the beam bridge's deck (or roadway). This causes the upper portion of the deck to shorten. The result of the compression on the upper portion of the deck causes tension in the lower portion of the deck. This tension causes the lower portion of the beam to lengthen.

(10) Take a two-by-four* and place it on top of two empty milk crates*— you've just created a crude beam bridge. Now place a 50-pound weight in the middle of it. Notice how the two-by-four bends. The top side is under compression and the bottom side is under tension. If you keep adding weight, eventually the two-by-four will break. Actually, the top side will buckle and the bottom side will snap.

> **two-by-four:** a piece of wood that is approximately 2 inches in depth and 4 inches in width
>
> **milk crates:** square boxes made of heavy plastic used to carry milk cartons

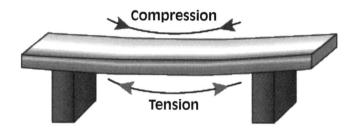

(11) Many beam bridges that you find on highway overpasses use concrete or steel beams to handle the load. The size of the beam, and in particular the height of the beam, controls the distance that the beam can span. By increasing the height of the beam, the beam has more material to dissipate the tension. To create very tall beams, bridge designers add supporting lattice work, or a **truss**, to the bridge's beam. This support truss adds rigidity to the existing beam, greatly increasing its ability to dissipate the compression and tension. Once the beam begins to compress, the force is dissipated through the truss.

(12) Despite the ingenious addition of a truss, the beam bridge is still limited in the distance it can span. As the distance increases, the size of the truss must also increase, until it reaches a point where the bridge's own weight is so large that the truss cannot support it.

Truss Strength

(13) A single beam spanning any distance experiences compression and tension. The very top of the beam experiences the most compression, and the very bottom of the beam experiences the most tension. The middle of the beam experiences very little compression or tension.

(14) If the beam were designed so that there was more material on the top and bottom, and less in the middle, it would be better able to handle the forces of compression and tension. (For this reason, I-beams are more rigid than simple rectangular beams.)

(15) A truss system takes this concept one step further. Think of one side of a truss bridge as a single beam. The center of the beam is made up of the diagonal members of the truss, while the top and bottom of the truss represent the top and bottom of the beam. Looking at a truss in this way, we can see that the top and bottom of the beam contain more material than its center (corrugated cardboard is very stiff for this reason).

(16) In addition to the above-mentioned effect of a truss system, there is another reason why a truss is more rigid than a single beam: A truss has the ability to dissipate a load through the truss work. The design of a truss, which is usually a variant of a triangle, creates both a very rigid structure and one that transfers the load from a single point to a considerably wider area.

The Arch Bridge

(17) An arch bridge is a semicircular structure with abutments on each end. The design of the arch, the semicircle, naturally diverts the weight from the bridge deck to the abutments*.

(18) Arch bridges are always under compression. The force of compression is pushed outward along the curve of the arch toward the abutments.

abutments: the place where two objects meet; the part of a structure that supports an arch

Compression lines

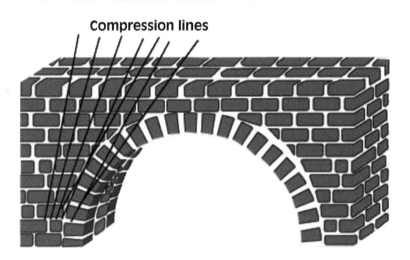

(19) The tension in an arch is negligible. The natural curve of the arch and its ability to dissipate the force outward greatly reduces the effects of tension on the underside of the arch. The greater the degree of curvature (the larger the semicircle of the arch), however, the greater the effects of tension on the underside.

(20) As mentioned, the shape of the arch itself is all that is needed to effectively dissipate the weight from the center of the deck to the abutments. As with the beam bridge, the limits of size will eventually overtake the natural strength of the arch.

(21) Arch types are few—after all, an arch is an arch is an arch. The only real subcategories come in the form of cosmetic design. There are, for example, Roman, Baroque, and Renaissance arches, all of which are architecturally different but structurally the same.

The Suspension Bridge

(22) A suspension bridge is one where cables (or ropes or chains) are strung across the river (or whatever the obstacle happens to be) and the deck is suspended from these cables. Modern suspension bridges have two tall towers through which the cables are strung. Thus, the towers are supporting the majority of the roadway's weight.

(23) The force of compression pushes down on the suspension bridge's deck, but because it is a suspended roadway, the cables transfer the compression to the towers, which dissipate the compression directly into the earth where they are firmly entrenched.

(24) The supporting cables, running between the two anchorages, are the lucky recipients of the tension forces. The cables are literally stretched from the weight of the bridge and its traffic as they run from anchorage to anchorage. The anchorages are also under tension, but since they, like the towers, are held firmly to the earth, the tension they experience is dissipated.

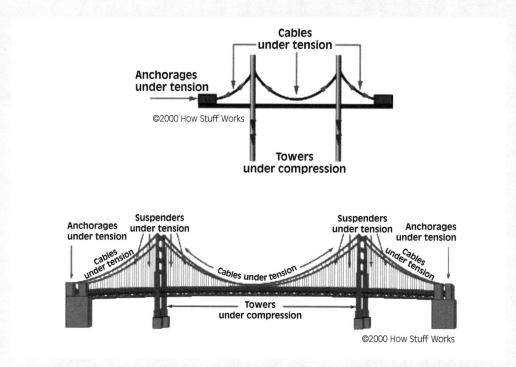

(25) Almost all suspension bridges have, in addition to the cables, a supporting truss system beneath the bridge deck (a **deck truss**). This helps to stiffen the deck and reduce the tendency of the roadway to sway and ripple.

Practice Activity: Making Text-to-Self Connections

Answer these questions that correspond to the stop signs in the reading.

1. Can I think of a bridge I go over or under every day or another one I know well? What does it look like?

   _____

2. Do I know what the three types of bridges in the reading look like? Have I seen all three?

   _____

3. When I think of the word *spring,* what do I think of? Does the "spring" example help me to understand the terms in this paragraph better?

   _____

4. Can I visualize what the words *buckling* and *snapping* mean as used here? What do they remind me of?

   _____

5. Have I seen a beam bridge before? Where?

   _____

6. Does this example of corrugated cardboard help my understanding? What do I picture?

   _____

7. Have I seen an arch bridge before? Where?

   _____

8. Have I seen a suspension bridge before? Where?

   _____

9. Thinking about my examples of a beam bridge, an arch bridge, and a suspension bridge, what can I determine about where each type of bridge is used (what it goes over) and where it is not used?

   _____

After Reading Strategy: Reviewing How Illustrations or Graphics Are Used in a Text

Graphics—illustrations, maps, charts, pictures, etc.—will often accompany a text. Sometimes, the graphic will simply "decorate" the text. For example, you may see a photo of something that seems to set the scene for a topic (for example, look at the unit opening photo on page 143). At other times, photos help to provide a visual of a person, event, or place in time that may make it easier of you to understand the reading. The photo from the movie *To Kill a Mockingbird* on page 132 is an example of this.

When you see a chart, a map, or a labeled illustration, especially if it occurs within the middle of the text, as you did in Reading 1, often it is a visual representation of something that is also being explained in writing. The author is using graphics to help make sure that you can understand the concept, as in the case of the different types of bridges. It's also worth noting that some scientific concepts are best explained with an illustration or diagram and often do not have much by way of explanation in the text.

As you encounter graphics within a reading, pay attention to whether they are there to provide a visual representation of what has been described in the text (to aid understanding), are provided to serve as the explanation of a concept (especially in science), or are there to break up the text AND give you a visual image of something that might help you understand the reading.

Some people understand graphics better; some understand the text more easily. However, good readers take full advantage of both text and graphics—they work back and forth between the graphics and the text.

Practice Activity: Reviewing How Illustrations or Graphics Are Used in a Text

Analyze illustrations and graphics by completing these tasks. Then share your findings with a partner.

1. Look through previous units in this book. Identify the purpose of each graphic included with a reading.

   _____

   _____

   _____

2. Now select one of your other textbooks, and go through a few units to determine how graphics are used in text. Decide whether most are included for "decoration," or if most seem to be included to help in understanding the content of the reading.

   _____

   _____

   _____

Practice Activity: Reading for the Big Picture

Put a check mark (✓) next to the statements that best reflect the main ideas.

1. _____ The main factor in determining the type of bridge to be built is the size of the obstacle to be spanned.

2. _____ The biggest difference between the three main types of bridges is the distance they can cover in a single span.

3. _____ A spring is a good example of buckling and snapping that the different bridge types need to deal with.

4. _____ There are only a few different types of arch bridges affected by tension and compression.

5. _____ Bridges support most of their weight with cables regardless of architectural design.

Paraphrasing to Simplify

Write a paraphrase that expresses the main points of the original without re-using too many words or phrases from the original.

1. A beam bridge is basically a rigid horizontal structure that is resting on two piers, or supports, one at each end.

   _____

   _____

   _____

2. To dissipate force is to spread it over a greater area so that no one spot has to bear the brunt of the concentrated force.

   _____

   _____

   _____

3. The supporting cables, running between the two anchorages, are the lucky recipients of the tension forces.

   _____

   _____

   _____

Writing Strategy: Writing Cause-and-Effect Statements

Many academic papers and class tests require you to examine the causes and effects of certain events. There can be one cause with several effects or several effects with one cause. These papers and test answers need to include sentences that explain how the causes and effects are related. There are certain words and phrases you can use to connect the causes to the effects.

as a result

because

cause

consequently

due to

effect

if . . . then

therefore

thus

If the brick is not to fall, then it must be sustained in its position in mid-air by a continuing equal and opposite upwards force or pull in the string.

The weight of the brick, like the weight of Newton's apple, is due to the effect of the earth's gravitational field upon its mass and it acts continually downwards.

Thus, when we hang a brick from the end of a piece of string, the string gets longer, and it is just this stretching which enable the string to pull upwards on the brick and so prevent it from falling.

The force of compression pushes down on the suspension bridge's deck, but because it is a suspended roadway, the cables transfer the compression to the towers, which dissipate the compression directly into the earth where they are firmly entrenched.

Using cause-and-effect statements is a good way to organize your writing and gives the reader an easy text pattern to follow.

Practice Activity: Using Cause-and-Effect Words and Phrases

For each topic, write a sentence using cause-and-effect words or phrases. The first one has been done for you as an example.

1. Give a reason for a bridge's failure.

   The Bay Bridge in San Francisco collapsed in 1989 because a large
   earthquake caused the bridge to shift.

2. Explain a country's successful economy.

   _____

   _____

3. Give reasons for the results of a science experiment.

   _____

   _____

4. Talk about the effects on a character at the end of a novel.

   _____

   _____

5. Discuss reasons why Pluto is (or is not) a planet.

   _____

   _____

6. Identify the effects of the fall of the Roman empire.

   _____

   _____

7. State the results of a sports game or event.

   _____

   _____

Short Writing Tasks

Write a response to each task following the directions given for length and source material.

Task 1 (Summary)

> Look again at Reading 1. Write a one-paragraph summary of the reading. Do not simply copy from the reading. A suggested approach is to make a list of key words and main ideas from the reading, and then to not look at the reading again. Review the box on page 15. Use only your notes as you prepare your own summary. Be sure to mention or cite your source. (Length: 5–7 sentences)

_____

_____

_____

_____

_____

_____

_____

Task 2 (Research)

> Reading 1 explains common types of bridges. Based on your instructor's guidelines, do some light research online or in a library to find an example of a famous bridge that is one of the three types. Describe the bridge and its type. Include information about its location, the obstacle it is spanning, its size, and what materials it is made from. Take notes in the space provided. Then write your paragraph on a separate piece of paper. (Length: 8–12 sentences)

_____

_____

_____

_____

_____

_____

Part 2: Structures

Getting Started

People take many common objects in their surroundings for granted; that is, they see those objects, but don't stop to think why those objects have the properties they do. Answer these questions with a partner.

1. How would you answer these questions: Why don't we fall through the floor? and How are solid objects (like a floor) able to resist a force (people walking on them)?

   _____

   _____

   _____

2. Do you think the answers to the questions posed in Question 1 are basically simple and easy to understand or difficult and complex?

   _____

   _____

   _____

3. Imagine you were a scientist who wanted to discover the answers to those asked in Question 1. How would you do so? Would you conduct experiments, think logically, or both? Or would you try some other method?

   _____

   _____

   _____

Reading 2 is from an engineering textbook called *Structures* by J.E. Gordon. It discusses the thought processes that led Robert Hooke, an English philosopher, scientist, and architect to an answer about how physical objects are able to resist forces. Called "England's Leonardo" (after Leonardo da Vinci) by some, Hooke is surprisingly less well known than the scientific principles he discovered.

When reading about scientific discoveries, writers may make passing reference to famous ideas, inventions, or events that the reader is expected to already know. The writer may also use new or technical vocabulary. However, it is possible that the reader is not familiar with some of these, either because of a lack of previous study in that area or because the ideas have been forgotten. However, because the ideas are now considered essential background knowledge, if you are not familiar with them, you should look for some information on them before you begin reading the text carefully. If you do not do this before, you will either have to interrupt your reading or have difficulty understanding new concepts that build on an understanding of previous ones.

Before Reading Strategy: Dealing with New or Technical Vocabulary

Sometimes your reading assignments will have technical words or words that are new to you. The key is to not stop reading when you encounter the words. Many times the definitions can be figured out from the context or the definition is given in the text. Writers sometimes use these strategies to help you figure out the definition.

Providing the Actual Definition

- after the *be* verb

    A span is the distance between two bridge supports, whether they are columns, towers, or the wall of a canyon.

- before, after, or between punctuation marks, such as commas, parentheses, colons, or dashes

    Bridges are truly ubiquitous—a natural part of everyday life.

    A bridge provides passage over some sort of obstacle: a river, a valley, a road, or a set of railroad tracks.

Giving Examples

- based on experience or experiments

  Thus, when we hang a brick from the end of a piece of string, the string gets longer, and it is just this stretching which enables the string to pull upwards on the brick and so prevent it from falling.

- based on fact

  The only real subcategories come in the form of cosmetic design. There are, for example, Roman, Baroque, and Renaissance arches, all of which are architecturally different but structurally the same.

Using Other Parts of the Sentence or Sentences before or after the Word

- before or after the word

  The biggest difference between the three is the distances they can cross in a single span. A span is the distance between two bridge supports, whether they are columns, towers or the wall of a canyon.

Using Signal Words

  . . . then it must somehow manage to produce a push or a pull which is exactly equal and opposite to the force which is being applied to it. That is, it has to resist all the pushes and pulls which may happen to arrive upon its doorstep by pushing and pulling back at them by just the right amount.

Using Synonyms

  In the case of the brick that hangs from a tree the load is supported by the tension in the string, in other words by a pull.

Practice Activity: Dealing with New or Technical Vocabulary

For each of the sentences from the reading, re-write the sentence to define or explain the word in bold. Use one of the strategies from the box.

1. This latter result is frequently **implicit** in the examination answers of engineering students.

   _____

   _____

2. Having hung a succession of weights upon them and measured the resulting deflections, he showed that the deflection in any given structure was usually **proportional** to the load.

   _____

   _____

3. The weight of the brick, like the weight of Newton's apple, is due to the effect of the earth's **gravitational field** upon its mass and it acts continually downwards.

   _____

   _____

Now write three sentences using words from your own field of study. Be prepared to read the sentences in a small group. Make sure your classmates, who may not be in the same field, will be able to understand your words.

4. _____

   _____

5. _____

   _____

6. _____

   _____

During Reading Strategy: Noting Important Information

Because there is so much reading to do in college, you often only have time to read the chapter or article once. It's important to notice important information and note it so that you can review it before tests or for other assignments. You can't mark too much, or else it would be like reading the entire chapter or article again. Some common ways to mark include highlighting, underlining, or circling key words or ideas. Another idea is to use sticky notes to mark the places with important information.

Important information to consider noting includes:

- main ideas (look for these in the first sentences of paragraphs)
- general conclusions (look for these in the last sentences of paragraphs)
- details (look for names, dates, and numbers as well as other unique information about a main idea)
- vocabulary (look for repeated, technical, or discipline-specific words)
- definitions (look for these by the first mention of a repeated word or by the technical or discipline-specific words)
- examples (look for these after signal words such as *for example, for instance,* or *to illustrate*)

You can also use a combination of marks. For example, you can circle vocabulary and highlight main ideas.

Practice Activity: Noting Important Information

As you read the text on pages 169–73, note the important information by highlighting, underlining, circling, tabbing, or using a combination of these methods. When you finish, answer these questions with a partner.

1. What methods did you choose to note the important information? Why did you choose these methods? Would you use the same methods again? Why or why not?

   _____

   _____

   _____

2. Did you highlight any of the same information? Discuss the similarities and differences. Remember there is no "right" answer, but it's sometimes helpful to talk about what other people consider important.

   _____

   _____

   _____

Vocabulary Power

There are a number of terms and phrases in this reading that you may encounter in other academic settings. Add at least five vocabulary items to your vocabulary notebook or log.

Match the words in bold from the reading on the left with a definition on the right.

1. _____ In the first place, Hooke realized that, if a material or a structure is able to resist a **load** [of any kind], it can only do so by pushing back at it with an equal and opposite force.

2. _____ If your feet push down on the floor, the floor must push up on your feet. If a cathedral pushes down on its **foundations**, the foundations must push up on the cathedral.

3. _____ However, a certain number of solids and near-solids, like putty and plasticine, do not recover completely but remain **distorted** when the load is taken off.

4. _____ How then can an **inert** or passive thing like a wall or a string—or, come to that, a bone or a steel girder or a cathedral—produce the large reactive forces which are needed?

5. _____ *All* materials and structures **deflect**, although to greatly varying extents, when they are loaded.

6. _____ Although *every* kind of solid changes its shape to some extent when a weight or other mechanical force is applied to it, the deflections that occur in practice **vary** enormously.

7. _____ Furthermore, within the **accuracy** of Hooke's measurements—which was not very good—most of these solids recovered from their original shape when the load which was causing the deflection was removed.

8. _____ Nowadays, and with **hindsight**, the idea that most materials and structures, not only machinery and bridges and buildings but also trees and animals and rocks and mountains and the round world itself, behave very much like springs may seem simple enough.

a. not moving; incapable of motion

b. weight to be supported or moved

c. preciseness

d. change

e. understanding something after it has happened; realizing a truth that was not perceived before

f. the lowest part of a structure that transfers the weight of the structure into the ground beneath it

g. turn or move something away from its original path or course

h. altered from the true or original state

Reading

Now, read the passage. Note important information by using a method from the box on page 166.

Hooke's Law

(1) How it is that any inanimate solid, such as steel or stone or timber or plastic, is able to resist a mechanical force at all—or even to sustain its own weight? This is, essentially, the problem of *Why don't we fall through the floor?* and the answer is by no means obvious. It lies at the root of the whole study of structures and is intellectually difficult. It [even] proved too difficult for Galileo, and the credit for the achievement of any real understanding of the problem is due to that very cantankerous* man Robert Hooke (1635–1702).

> **cantankerous:** bad tempered, disagreeable

(2) In the first place, Hooke realized that, if a material or a structure is able to resist a load [of any kind], it can only do so by pushing back at it with an equal and opposite force. If your feet push down on the floor, the floor must push up on your feet. If a cathedral pushes down on its foundations, the foundations must push up on the cathedral. This is implicit in Newton's third law of motion, which . . . is about action and reaction being equal and opposite.

(3) In other words, a force cannot just get lost. Always and whatever happens, every force must be balanced and reacted by another equal and opposite force at every point throughout a structure. This is true for any kind of structure, however small and simple or however large and complicated it may be. It is true, not only for floors and cathedrals, but also for bridges and airplanes and balloons and furniture and lions and tigers and cabbages and earthworms.

(4) If this condition is not fulfilled, that is to say if all the forces are not in equilibrium or balance with each other, then either the structure will break or else the whole affair must take off, like a rocket, and end up somewhere in outer space. This latter result is frequently implicit in the examination answers of engineering students.

(5) Let us consider for a moment the simplest possible sort of structure. Suppose that we hang a weight, such as an ordinary brick, from some support—which might be the branch of a tree—by means of a piece of string (Figure 1). The weight of the brick, like the

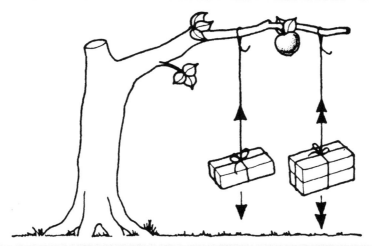

Figure 1. The weight of the brick, acting downwards, must be supported by an equal and opposite upward pull or tension in the string.

weight of Newton's apple, is due to the effect of the earth's gravitational field* upon its mass and it acts continually downwards. If the brick is not to fall, then it must be sustained in its position in mid-air by a continuing equal and opposite upwards force or pull in the string. If the string is too weak, so that it cannot produce an upward force equal to the weight of the brick, then the string will break and the brick will fall to the ground—again like Newton's apple.*

gravitational field: the area around a large body that causes the attraction of other large bodies

(6)   However, if our string is a strong one, so that we are able to hang not one, but two, bricks from it, then the string will now have to produce twice as much upward force; that is, enough to support both bricks. And so on, of course, for any other variations of the load. Moreover, the load does not have to be a "dead" weight* such as a brick; forces arising from any other cause, such as the pressure of the wind, must be resisted by the same sort of reaction.

Newton's apple: Sir Isaac Newton formed the theory of gravity after seeing an apple fall from a tree.

dead weight: very heavy motionless body

(7)   In the case of the brick that hangs from a tree the load is supported by the tension in the string, in other words by a pull. In many structures, such as buildings, the load is carried in compression, that is by pushing. In both cases the general principles are the same. Thus if any structural system is to do its job—that is to say, if the load is supported in a satisfactory way so that nothing very much happens—then it must somehow manage to produce a push or a pull which is exactly equal and opposite to the force which is being applied to it. That is, it has to resist all the pushes and pulls which may happen to arrive upon its doorstep by pushing and pulling back at them by just the right amount.

(8) This is all very well and it is generally fairly easy to see why a load pushes or pulls on a structure. The difficulty is to see why the structure should push or pull back at the load. . . .

(9) How then can an inert or passive thing like a wall or a string—or, come to that, a bone or a steel girder* or a cathedral—produce the large reactive forces which are needed?

steel girder: piece of metal used as support in bridges

(10) By about 1676 Hooke saw clearly that, not only must solids resist weights or other mechanical loads by pushing back at them, but also that

1. Every kind of solid *changes its shape*—by stretching or contracting itself—when a mechanical force is applied to it.
2. It is this change of shape which enables the solid to do the pushing back.

(11) Thus, when we hang a brick from the end of a piece of string, the string gets longer, and it is just this stretching which enables the string to pull upwards on the brick and so prevent it from falling. *All* materials and structures deflect, although to greatly varying extents, when they are loaded.

(12) It is important to realize that it is perfectly normal for any and every structure to deflect in response to a load. Unless this deflection is too large for the purposes of the structure, it is not in any way a fault but rather an essential characteristic without which no structure would be able to work. *The science of elasticity is about the interactions between forces and deflections in materials and structures.*

(13) Although *every* kind of solid changes its shape to some extent when a weight or other mechanical force is applied to it, the deflections that occur in practice vary enormously. With a thing like a plant or a piece of rubber the deflections are often very large and easily seen, but when we put ordinary loads on hard substances like metal or concrete or bone the deflections are sometimes very small indeed. Although such movements are often far too small to see with the naked eye, they always exist and are perfectly real, even though we may need special appliances in order to measure them. When you climb the tower of a cathedral it becomes shorter, as a result of your added weight, by a very, very tiny amount, but it really does become shorter. As a matter of fact, masonry* is really more flexible than you

masonry: building structures with separate pieces held together with mortar

might think, as one can see by looking at the four principal columns that support the tower of Salisbury Cathedral: they are all quite noticeably bent.

(14) Hooke made a further important step in his reasoning which, even nowadays, some people find difficult to follow. He realized that, when any structure deflects under load in the way we have been talking about, the material from which it is made is itself also stretched or contracted, internally, throughout all its parts and in due proportion, down to a very fine scale—as we know nowadays, down to a molecular scale. Thus, when we deform a stick or a steel spring—say by bending it—the atoms and molecules of which the material is made have to move further apart, or else squash closer together, when the material as a whole is stretched or compressed.

(15) As we also know nowadays, the chemical bonds which join the atoms to each other, and so hold the solid together, are very strong and stiff indeed. So when the material as a whole is stretched or compressed this can only be done by stretching or compressing many millions of strong chemical bonds which vigorously resist being deformed, even to a very small extent. Thus these bonds produce the required large forces of reaction.

(16) Although Hooke knew nothing in detail about chemical bonds and not very much about atoms and molecules, he understood perfectly well that something of this kind was happening within the fine structure of the material, and he set out to determine what might be the nature of the macroscopic relationship between forces and deflections in solids.

(17) He tested a variety of objects made from various materials and having various geometrical forms, such as springs and wires and beams. Having hung a succession of weights upon them and measured the resulting deflections, he showed that the deflection in any given structure was usually proportional to the load. That is to say, a load of 200 pounds would cause twice as much deflection as a load of 100 pounds and so on.

(18) Furthermore, within the accuracy of Hooke's measurements—which was not very good—most of these solids recovered from their original shape when the load which was causing the deflection was removed. In fact he could usually go on loading and unloading structures of this kind indefinitely without causing any permanent change of shape. Such behaviour is called *elastic* and is common. The word is often associated with rubber bands and underclothes, but it is just as applicable to steel and stone and

brick and to biological substances like wood and bone and tendon. It is in this wider sense that engineers generally use it.

(19) However, a certain number of solids and near-solids, like putty and plasticine, do not recover completely but remain distorted when the load is taken off. This kind of behavior is called *plastic*. The word is by no means confined to the materials from which ashtrays are usually made but is also applied to clay and to soft metals. Such plastic substances shade off into things like butter and porridge and treacle.* Furthermore, many of the materials that Hooke considered to be elastic turn out to be imperfectly so when tested by more accurate modern methods.

treacle: molasses, in British English

(20) However, as a broad generalization, Hooke's observations remain true and still provide the basis of the modern science of elasticity. Nowadays, and with hindsight, the idea that most materials and structures, not only machinery and bridges and buildings but also trees and animals and rocks and mountains and the round world itself, behave very much like springs may seem simple enough—perhaps blindingly obvious—but, from his diary, it is clear that to get thus far cost Hooke great mental effort and many doubts. It is perhaps one of the great intellectual achievements of history.

(21) After he had tried out his ideas on Sir Christopher Wren in a series of private arguments, Hooke published his experiments in 1679 in a paper called "De potential restitutiva or of spring." This paper contained the famous statement "ut tension sic vis" ("as the extension, so the force"). This principle has been known for three hundred years as "Hooke's law."

After Reading Strategy: Integrating Information from Two Sources

In academic courses, it is common to synthesize or integrate information from different sources. In other words, you will have to realize how two readings may be related and make connections between them.

There are several things you can do to connect two readings:

- Relate the materials to your own prior knowledge, experience, and research.

- Use class notes from lectures.

- Talk with your teachers and classmates to gather additional information.

- Create graphic organizers so you can see what the two readings have in common or what their differences are, what opinions they share and which they disagree on, or what results are similar or different.

- Note the organization, tone, and sources the two pieces use.

- Note what vocabulary the two pieces share and use often.

- Write paraphrases and summaries of the main ideas from each and compare them.

By using one or more of these strategies, you can prepare yourself to answer a test question or write a research paper using the two readings.

Practice Activity: Integrating Information from Two Sources

Complete the Venn Diagram for the two readings. On the right side, write key words and notes that Reading 1 gives about how bridges are built. On the left side, write key words and notes that Reading 2 discusses about that same topic. Then, list key words and notes from both readings where the circles overlap.

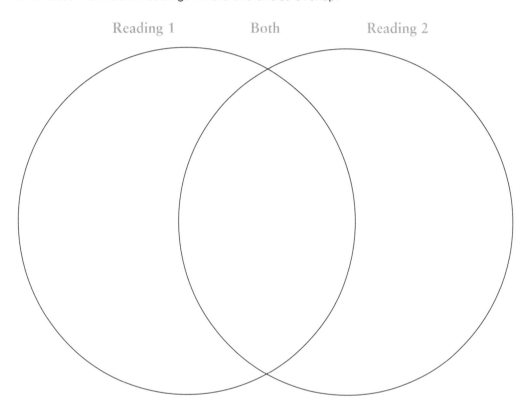

Reading 1   Both   Reading 2

Write a summary about how structures are built and integrate information from both readings.

_____

_____

_____

_____

_____

_____

Practice Activity: Reading for the Big Picture

Put a check mark (✓) next to the statements that best reflect the main ideas.

1. _____ Hooke's law is easily understood now, but it was a very difficult problem during the 1600s.

2. _____ Hooke's law explains the relationship between force and the materials that force is applied to.

3. _____ A solid that recovers its original shape after force has been applied is said to be elastic.

4. _____ There really isn't any such thing as a "solid" material; all materials have some plasticity.

5. _____ Heavy materials are stronger than light ones, and this affects the plasticity.

Paraphrasing to Simplify

Write a paraphrase that expresses the main points of the original without re-using too many words or phrases from the original.

1. This is all very well and it is generally fairly easy to see why a load pushes or pulls on a structure. The difficulty is to see why the structure should push or pull back at the load.

   _____

   _____

   _____

2. Although *every* kind of solid changes its shape to some extent when a weight or other mechanical force is applied to it, the deflections that occur in practice vary enormously.

   _____

   _____

   _____

3. Nowadays, and with hindsight, the idea that most materials and structures, not only machinery and bridges and buildings but also trees and animals and rocks and mountains and the round world itself, behave very much like springs may seem simple enough—perhaps blindingly obvious—but, from his diary, it is clear that to get thus far cost Hooke great mental effort and many doubts. It is perhaps one of the great intellectual achievements of history.

   _____

   _____

   _____

Writing Strategy: Writing about Evidence or Support

Students studying the sciences often have to use the scientific method—techniques to learn about previous studies and add new ideas. These students need to gather data and explain it without being biased or giving their own opinions. Even students in the humanities and social sciences need to be able to support their statements. Three good strategies you can use to support your evidence include quoting others, giving facts, and using statistics.

Quotations: statements given by someone else, usually an expert in the field.

> "There are very few books where the characters are unforgettable, the story is suspenseful in the best kind of dramatic way, and it has a social message without being preachy," says Mary McDonagh Murphy, author of a new book of interviews of famous folk talking about how *Mockingbird* changed them, and changed the country.

Facts: statements that are objective and have been or can be proven

> Every kind of solid *changes its shape*—by stretching or contracting itself—when a mechanical force is applied to it.
>
> . . . a load of 200 pounds would cause twice as much deflection as a load of 100 pounds and so on.

Statistics: numbers and figures that can be explained in writing or in graphs

> New York has more than 17,000 bridges and 44% of them are owned by the New York State Department of Transportation. Approximately 50% are owned by municipalities, and the rest are owned by state and local authorities, commissions, and railroads. (www.nysdot.gov/bridgedata)

You could include this graph about the bridge conditions in New York.

NYS Highway Bridge Conditions

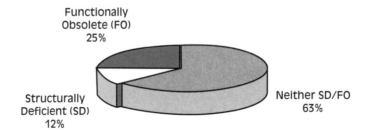

Functionally Obsolete (FO) 25%

Structurally Deficient (SD) 12%

Neither SD/FO 63%

A piece of writing to accompany the statistics will look like this:

> Based upon data submitted to the FHWA in April 2009, about 12 percent of the highway bridges in New York State are classified, under the broad federal standards, as structurally deficient and about 25 percent are classified as functionally obsolete. Those classifications do not mean the bridges are unsafe, rather that they would require repairs or modifications to restore their condition or improve their functionality. Again, if a bridge is deemed unsafe, it is closed to traffic. These statistics help highlight bridges that should be considered for further review, maintenance, repair, rehabilitation or replacement.
>
> From: New York State Department of Transportation, Copyright 1999–2010. Accessed on October 30, 2010, at https://www.nysdot.gov/bridgedata.

Practice Activity: Writing about Facts and Statistics

Look at the chart, and write a few sentences about the statistics. Include cause-and-effect statements when you can make guesses about what this data may cause or what effects it may have.

Exhibit 2–13 Bridges by Owner, 1996–2002

Number of Bridges by Year				
Owner	1996	1998	2000	2002
Federal	6,171	7,748	8,221	9,371
State	273,198	273,897	277,106	280,266
Local	299,078	298,222	298,889	299,354
Private/Railroad	2,378	2,278	2,299	1,502
Unknown/Unclassified	1,037	1,131	415	1,214
Total	581,862	583,276	586,930	591,707

_____

_____

_____

_____

_____

_____

Your Active Vocabulary in the Real World

Vocabulary is important. Some words are useful for your speaking or for your writing, but other words are useful for your reading or your listening. For each word, decide how you think you will probably need this word for your English. Put a check mark (✓) under the correct ways you think you are likely to need the word. It is possible to have a check mark in more than one column.

	YOUR VOCABULARY	I need to be able to use this word in WRITING.	I need to be able to use this word in SPEAKING.	I need to understand this word in READING.	I need to understand this word in LISTENING.
1.	complicated				
2.	concept				
3.	crucial				
4.	detect				
5.	deviation				
6.	firmly				
7.	likely				
8.	particular				
9.	tendency				
10.	worth				

Rapid Vocabulary Review

From the three answers on the right, circle the one that best explains, is an example of, or combines with vocabulary word on the left as it is used in this unit.

Vocabulary	Answers		
Synonyms			
1. sway	find	move	try
2. essentially	basically	loudly	unusually
3. weak	not below	not horizontal	not strong
4. an obstacle	a barrier	a beam	a brick
5. stiff	circular	hard	quick
6. transfer	change places	keep moving	run out of
7. a log	meat	plastic	wood
8. a cathedral	a big bridge	a big church	a big dam
9. the pinnacle	the story	the top	the year
10. ubiquitous	almost dead	everywhere	near an ocean
11. a valley	between 2 buildings	between 2 mountains	between 2 people
12. a stream	like a friend	like a hill	like a river
Combinations and Associations			
13. ____ likely to	is	goes	sees
14. X is ____ up of Y	done	made	taken
15. the type ____	at	into	of
16. a diagonal ____	floor	line	person
17. up ____ 100	can	next	to
18. a branch of a ____	bridge	house	tree
19. fulfill a ____	condition	meeting	talent
20. due ____ the weather	for	in	to

⇨✕⊐ Synthesizing: Writing Projects

In-Class Assignments	Outside Assignments
Loads and Bridges	The Arch or the Dome?
Imagine you are taking a test. Use your understanding of Hooke's Law to explain the cause and effect: What do civil engineers who design bridges need to understand about loads? **Suggested Length:** 300 words **Preparation:** none	Research either arches or domes in more detail. Write an essay that outlines their appearance in history and how they work. List famous examples. Include illustrations. **Suggested Length:** 800 words **Preparation:** Light research in a library or online
Bridge Designing	Online Research: Key Scientific Discoveries
Integrating the material from the readings with your own ideas and experience, design a bridge for your school's campus. Describe its location, the obstacle it spans, and its design. Support your ideas with facts when possible. Make a short presentation to your class. **Suggested Length:** 500 words **Preparation:** none	Find the story behind a key scientific discovery. Choose from one of these or use your own idea (but check with your instructor first): • gravity • electricity • longitude • that the earth is round • that the earth revolves around the sun Write an essay summarizing your research. Integrate material from at least two sources. **Suggested Length:** 1,000 words **Preparation:** Light research in a library or online

Vocabulary Log

To increase your vocabulary knowledge, write a definition or translation for each vocabulary item. Then write an original phrase, sentence, or note that will help you remember the vocabulary item.

Vocabulary Item	Definition or Translation	Your Original Phrase, Sentence, or Note
1. climb	to go up	a cat climbed a tree
2. a principle		
3. inert		
4. as a matter of fact		
5. hindsight		
6. string		
7. vigorously		
8. lengthen		
9. arise		
10. a deck		
11. a bone		
12. resist		
13. ingenious		
14. stretch		

Vocabulary Item	Definition or Translation	Your Original Phrase, Sentence, or Note
15. enable		
16. a variant		
17. tiny		
18. an atom		
19. a molecule		
20. nowadays		
21. semicircle		
22. a brick		
23. a chain		
24. divert		
25. a diary		

6 Political Science: Early Presidents and Their Decisions

Political science is a field of study that examines many facets of a government, including its laws, lands, and leaders. One leader in the United States is the president. Throughout the country's history, there have been many presidents, and they have had many differences. One thing they have all had in common is the challenge of making difficult decisions. This unit explores two presidents and the decisions they made when they were serving the country.

Part 1: George Washington

Getting Started

On April 30, 1789, George Washington was sworn in as the first president of the United States when the country was only 13 years old. Current presidents have a detailed job description and have had other presidents to learn from. George Washington did not have that same opportunity. Answer these questions with a partner.

1. What kinds of things do you think Washington had to think about as the first U.S. president?

   _____

   _____

   _____

2. What types of decisions do presidents or other leaders have to make? Which do you think are the most challenging?

   _____

   _____

   _____

3. Have you served as an officer in a club or organization? If so, what was difficult? What things do leaders of groups need to do?

   _____

   _____

   _____

Reading 1 is from a book titled *Founding Fathers* and is about the most important people involved in the founding of the United States. The book discusses Benjamin Franklin, Thomas Jefferson, and George Washington, the three men shown on page 185. The book discusses George Washington's progression to the presidency and his decision to leave office, including his Farewell Address.

Students often have a lot of reading to do; some readings will be longer and more detailed than others. Successful readers plan a little before they read to get some understanding of the passage's level of difficulty and of the time it may take to read it. **The readings in this unit are purposefully challenging and difficult so that they better replicate authentic university reading assignments.** Just like university assignments, they contain a lot of references to people and events that you may not be familiar with. Which ones do you need to know to understand the reading?

Before Reading Strategy: Gauging Difficulty and Time Required

Readings that contain a lot of new or specialized vocabulary—or a lot of new or detailed information—can be more difficult to read than students first expect—even if the reading is only a few pages long. As discussed in Unit 1, skimming can give you a sense of how difficult a passage might be. However, there are certain specific things you can do to gauge the difficulty and determine how much time you need for successful comprehension.

1. Look at the length of the reading. Think about how much time it would take you to read a relatively easy text of this length on a topic you're familiar with or in your native language. Understand that you may need more time than this.

2. Skim the reading to get a sense of how much new or technical vocabulary it includes. Do you know most of the words? If not, estimate how much time you will need to look up important vocabulary.

3. Look at the average sentence length in the reading. Decide if the longer sentences are more complex grammatically and will require re-reading to completely understand. Think about whether the complexity of the writing will take your focus from the topic.

4. Look a little more carefully, especially in a reading where there are no subtitles or headings, to see if there are several "parts" to the topic. For example, does the text deal with an issue's past and then move on to discuss its future? Does the text give a definition or description and then describe a process? Does the text describe a process and then give ideas for improvement? Does the text give ideas for something, and then against it? If possible, mark the text where the main topic breaks into sections or subtopics. Then you can take each section separately, which will make reading less overwhelming.

Practice Activity: Gauging Difficulty and Time Required

Find out how difficult Reading 1 will be for you and how much time it will take so that you can plan your reading time. Answer these questions about each step in the process.

1. How long is the reading (how many pages or paragraphs)? _____

   How many minutes would you need to read an article of this length in your native language? _____

   Do you need more or less time for this article? How many more minutes do you need? _____

2. Do you know most of the words or are there technical or new vocabulary words? _____

   After circling or highlighting the unknown words, what percentage of them do you need to look up? _____

   Since important words are often repeated, how much time do you need to look those up? _____

3. Are there many long sentences? After reading one paragraph, what is the average sentence length? _____

   Are the sentences complex in grammar or detail? Can you easily identify the subjects and verbs? _____

   Do you need more time to focus on the topic or will the sentence length slow your understanding? _____

   How much extra time should you schedule? _____

4. How many parts does this reading have? _____

   Where does each begin? _____

   What does each part cover? _____

   Should you read the parts in one sitting or should you break it into more than one? _____

5. Estimate a final number of minutes you need for this reading. _____

During Reading Strategy: Creating Visual and Sensory Images

Good readers purposefully create mental images as they read. Images are useful in helping readers to immerse themselves in a given time period or place, but they also help the reader engage with the material and to remember it better.

Creating visual images of what you are reading can help you focus on important details and develop a stronger overall sense of the purpose of the reading. There are many types of readings where visual and sensory imaging works, but it can be particularly useful when reading about a different period of time or about a different place. Remember that for some reading passages it may help to think about how things might smell or feel as well as how they might look.

Practice Activity: Creating Visual and Sensory Images

As you read, try imagining these images. Make notes here. Share your images with a partner.

1. Imagine life in the 1790s in any country. What did a city look like then? How were people dressed? Can you picture America?

   _____

   _____

2. The reading also references other dates—1755, 1776, and 1789. Try to visualize life in 1755 and compare it to your image of 1789. What's different? What's the same? Why?

   _____

   _____

3. Paragraph 2 describes a battle. What other senses can you use to imagine this event? What might you smell? What might you hear? What might you feel?

   _____

   _____

4. The reading talks about the shock of finding out that the only leader Americans had ever known was not going to be their leader anymore. Imagine how you would feel if you were in a situation that was new to you and suddenly everything was going to change? What emotions would you have?

   _____

   _____

🏋️ Vocabulary Power

There are a number of terms and phrases in this reading that you may encounter in other academic settings. Add at least five vocabulary items to your vocabulary notebook or log.

Match the words in bold from the reading on the left with a definition on the right.

1. _____ . . . the **distinction** between his human qualities and his heroic achievements impossible to delineate.

2. _____ During Gen. Edward Braddock's ill-fated **expedition** against the French outside Pittsburgh in 1755. . . .

3. _____ At Yorktown in 1781, he had insisted on standing atop a parapet for a full fifteen minutes during an artillery attack, bullets and shrapnel flying all about him, **defying** aides who tried to pull him down before he had properly surveyed the field of action.

4. _____ The only serious **contender** for primacy was Benjamin Franklin, but just before his death in 1790, Franklin himself acknowledged Washington's supremacy.

5. _____ His **commanding** presence had been the central feature in every major event of the revolutionary era. . . .

6. _____ If there were a Mount Olympus in the new American republic, all the lesser gods were gathered farther down the **slope.**

7. _____ Every major newspaper in the country reprinted the article over the **ensuing** weeks. . . .

8. _____ And in the late nineteenth century the Congress made its reading a **mandatory** ritual on Washington's birthday.

a. getting attention

b. happening after

c. required

d. difference

e. resisting

f. trip taken for a specific reason

g. side of a hill or mountain

h. a competitor

Reading

Now, read the passage. Try to create images of time and place as you read. Also, because this is a difficult reading, put an X next to the lines that have information you aren't sure you understand. You will use these when you practice the After Reading Strategy on page 194.

The Farewell

(1) Throughout the first half of the 1790s, the closest approximation to a self-evident truth in American politics was George Washington. A legend in his own time, Americans had been describing Washington as "the Father of the Country" since 1776—which is to say, before there was even a country. By the time he assumed the presidency in 1789— no other candidate was even thinkable—the mythology surrounding Washington's reputation had grown like ivy over a statue, effectively covering the man with an aura of omnipotence, rendering the distinction between his human qualities and his heroic achievements impossible to delineate.

(2) Some of the most incredible stories also happened to be true. During General Edward Braddock's ill-fated expedition* against the French outside Pittsburgh in 1755, a young Washington had joined with Daniel Boone to rally the survivors, despite having two horses shot out from under him and multiple bullet holes piercing his coat and creasing his pants. At Yorktown in 1781, he had insisted on standing atop a parapet* for a full fifteen minutes during an artillery attack, bullets and shrapnel flying all about him, defying aides

> **Braddock's ill-fated expedition:** Braddock attempted to capture the French Fort Duquesne during the French and Indian War
>
> **parapet:** a low wall

who tried to pull him down before he had properly surveyed the field of action. When Washington spoke of destiny, people listened.

(3) If there were a Mount Olympus* in the new American republic, all the lesser gods were gathered farther down the slope. The only serious contender for primacy was Benjamin Franklin, but just before his death in 1790, Franklin himself acknowledged Washington's supremacy.

> **Mount Olympus:** the highest mountain in Greece; home to the gods in Greek mythology

George Washington during the French and Indian War.

(4) In the America of the 1790s, Washington's image was everywhere, in paintings, prints, lockets; on coins, silverware, plates, and common household items. His commanding presence had been the central feature in every major event of the revolutionary era: he was the linchpin of the Continental Army throughout eight long years of desperate fighting from 1775 to 1783; he was the presiding officer at the Constitutional Convention in 1787; and he was the first and only chief executive of the fledgling federal government since 1789. He was America's one and only indispensable character. Washington was the core of gravity that prevented the American Revolution from flying off into random orbits, the stable center around which the revolutionary energies formed. As one popular toast* of the day put it, he was "the man who unites all hearts."

toast: words said in honor of someone

(5) Then, all of a sudden, on September 19, 1796, an article addressed to "the PEOPLE of the United States" appeared on the inside pages of the *American Daily Advertiser*, Philadelphia's major newspaper. The conspicuous austerity of the announcement was matched by its calculated simplicity. It began: "Friends, and Fellow Citizens: The period for a new election of a Citizen, to Administer the Executive government of the United States, being not far distant . . . it appears to me proper, especially as it may conduce to a more distinct expression of the public voice,* that I should now apprise you of the resolutions I have formed, to decline being considered among the number of those, out of whom a choice is to be made." It ended, again in a gesture of ostentatious moderation, with the unadorned signature: "G. Washington, United States."

public voice: what the people of a city or country want

(6) Every major newspaper in the country reprinted the article over the ensuing weeks, though only one, the *Courier of New Hampshire*, gave it the title that would echo through the ages—"Washington's Farewell Address." Contemporaries began to debate its contents almost immediately, and a lively (and ultimately silly) argument soon ensued about whether Washington or Hamilton actually wrote it. Over a longer stretch of time, the Farewell Address achieved transcendental status, ranking alongside the Declaration of Independence and the Gettysburg Address as a seminal statement of America's abiding principles. Its Olympian tone made it a perennial touchstone* at those political occasions requiring platitudinous wisdom.* And in the late nineteenth century the Congress made its reading a mandatory ritual on

perennial touchstone: a basis that exists all the time

platitudinous wisdom: dull or boring intelligence

Washington's birthday. Meanwhile, several generations of historians, led by students of American diplomacy, have made the interpretation of the Farewell Address into a cottage industry* of its own, building up a veritable mountain of commentary around what it may implying about an isolationist foreign policy and a bipartisan brand of American statecraft.*

cottage industry: home-based rather than factory-based

statecraft: the management of government matters

(7) But in the heat of the moment, none of these subsequent affectations or interpretations mattered much, if at all. What did matter, indeed struck most readers as the only thing that truly mattered, was that George Washington was retiring. The constitutional significance of the decision, of course, struck home immediately, signaling as it did Washington's voluntary surrender of the presidency after two terms, thereby setting the precedent that held firm until 1940, when Franklin Delano Roosevelt broke it. (It was reaffirmed in 1951 with passage of the 22nd Amendment.) But even that landmark precedent, so crucial in establishing the republican* principle of rotation in office, paled in comparison to an even more elemental political and psychological realization.

republican: government that has a chief of state, usually a president

(8) For twenty years, over the entire life span of the revolutionary war and the experiment with republican government, Washington had stood at the helm of the ship of state. Now he was sailing off into the sunset. The precedent he was setting may have seemed uplifting in retrospect, but at the time the glaring and painful reality was that the United States without Washington was itself unprecedented. The Farewell Address, as several commentators have noted, was an oddity in that it was not really an address: it was never delivered as a speech. It should, by all rights, be called the Farewell Letter, for it was in form and tone an open letter to the American people, telling them they were now on their own.

After Reading Strategy: Re-Reading

Re-reading is one of the most popular strategies readers use when they are reading a difficult text or are struggling to understand a new concept. Re-reading does not mean reading the entire passage again. Rather, it means going back to the part of the text where you stopped understanding and trying to read it again. Sometimes this means you only need to re-read a sentence, but sometimes you may need to start again at the beginning to find out where you stopped understanding.

When you re-read, you usually do read something more slowly, and often it's just the fact of slowing down that makes the text easier to understand the next time around. Also, because you have read the content once, you now already know basically where the reading is going and already understand some parts of it, which means you are just filling in the pieces now instead of attempting a global understanding.

Re-reading helps with vocabulary too because you already know which words you don't know and so you are prepared when you read them the next time, meaning you can now focus on looking more at the context to see if that will help you understand unfamiliar words.

Remember that re-reading does not just mean reading something one more time. For some readings, you may need to read different parts three or four times. Don't get discouraged!

It is difficult to know in advance what parts or how much you will have to re-read. Every piece of text will be different.

Practice Activity: Re-Reading

Re-read Reading 1 in its entirety. This time, read more slowly and deliberately. On this second pass through the reading, if you find that you understand something now that you didn't understand before, erase the X or cross it off.

1. Now re-read the lines/sections that still have X marks in the margin. If necessary, go back a sentence or two to try to get more of a context for the parts you don't understand.

2. If some of the items you did not understand are references to particular people or historical events, ask your teacher or go online to find out more about these items.

Practice Activity: Reading for the Big Picture

Put a check mark (✓) next to the statements that best reflect the main ideas.

1. _____ Washington's most serious contender was Braddock.

2. _____ Washington's farewell was surprising to everyone.

3. _____ In his farewell address, Washington wrote he didn't want to be considered for the presidency.

4. _____ The Farewell Address was published for many weeks and is still read today.

5. _____ Arguments about Washington's letter include who the actual author really was.

Paraphrasing to Simplify

Write a paraphrase that expresses the main points of the original without re-using too many words or phrases from the original.

1. Washington was the core of gravity that prevented the American Revolution from flying off into random orbits, the stable center around which the revolutionary energies formed.

   _____

   _____

   _____

2. Every major newspaper in the country reprinted the article over the ensuing weeks, though only one, the *Courier of New Hampshire*, gave it the title that would echo through the ages—"Washington's Farewell Address."

   _____

   _____

   _____

3. For twenty years, over the entire life span of the revolutionary war and the experiment with republican government, Washington had stood at the helm of the ship of state.

   _____

   _____

   _____

Writing Strategy: Unity and Coherence

Good writing contains many paragraphs about a topic. Writers need to make sure their paragraphs are unified. Unity is when a paragraph has one main idea and all the sentences are about that main idea.

Good paragraphs are also coherent. Coherence means that the sentences go well together and that each flows into the next one.

To make sure each paragraph is unified and coherent, use these strategies:

- Do not change the topic or main idea.

- Repeat key nouns and/or use consistent pronouns

- Link sentences together with transitions.

- Logically organize your main idea and details.

Practice Activity: Unity and Coherence

Read these sentences from a paragraph about the capital being named after George Washington. Put them in the order you think is best by labeling each 1 through 6. Then answer the questions on page 197.

_____ Americans were painfully aware that his life was rapidly ticking away.

_____ It was to be the nation's paramount unifying symbol, the brick-and-marble embodiment of its ideals and aspiration.

_____ The new capital would offer proof to the outside world that the United States was here to stay.

_____ "While we had a Washington and his virtues to cement and guard the union, it might be safe; but, when he shall leave us, who would inherit _his virtues, and possess his influence?_"

_____ He was fifty-eight years old in 1790, elderly by the standards of the time, and his health was a constant worry.

_____ For the time being, this unique role was filled by the most trusted man in the United States: President George Washington.

1. Is the paragraph about only one topic? If not, how could you unify it?

   _____

   _____

2. Are key nouns repeated? Are there any places where you'd repeat a noun?

   _____

   _____

3. Are any pronouns used? Would you replace any of them?

   _____

   _____

4. Are the sentences linked with transitions? Where would you add others?

   _____

   _____

5. Are the sentences in a logical order? Is there another option? If so, how can you strengthen coherence so there is only one logical order?

   _____

   _____

Short Writing Tasks

Write your response to each task following the directions given for length and source material.

Task 1 (Summary)

Look again at Reading 1. Write a one-paragraph summary of the reading. Do not simply copy from the reading. A suggested approach is to make a list of key words and main ideas from the reading, and then to not look at the reading again. Review the box on page 15. Use only your notes as you prepare your own summary. Be sure to mention or cite your source. (Length: 5–7 sentences)

_____

_____

_____

_____

_____

_____

_____

Task 2 (Research)

Was Washington's decision to leave the presidency ultimately good for the new nation of the United States of America? Explain with information you know about American history from activating your prior knowledge or what you learned after the reading the passage. Take notes in the space provided. Then write your paragraphs on a separate piece of paper. (Length: 8–12 sentences)

_____

_____

_____

_____

_____

_____

_____

Part 2: Thomas Jefferson

Getting Started

Thomas Jefferson was the third president of the United States. He was one of the writers of the Declaration of Independence and fought for independence from the British Empire. One of Jefferson's most notable achievements was expanding the United States. He supported the Lewis and Clark Expedition and he made the Louisiana Purchase.

1. What kinds of things do presidents spend money on? Which of those do you think are the most important? The least important?

   _____

   _____

   _____

2. What things would you spend money on if you were President of the United States? What would help you make your decisions?

   _____

   _____

   _____

Reading 2 is from a book titled *American Creation* and is written by the same author as Reading 1. This book discusses the beginnings of the United States in more depth. The topics include Thomas Jefferson and his decision to make the Louisiana Purchase, which greatly increased the size of the United States.

Because some academic readings are long, it's a good idea to break them into smaller parts and to develop strategies for getting through longer pieces of text and understanding them.

Before Reading Strategy: Breaking a Reading into Manageable Chunks

When you are assigned a long reading or one that you know is going to be full of new information that is difficult, one of the best strategies is to divide the material into more manageable chunks.

You might break the reading up several ways. For example, you may decide that several pages are a manageable chunk. Or you may divide the text into sections or paragraphs. Do whatever is useful for you. The purpose of this is to help you develop a good understanding of each chunk before you go on to the next chunk.

Breaking a reading into pieces also allows you to do some outside research. For example, you may need to search for unfamiliar historical names or events online before you read further, or you may need to look up some new vocabulary words. Make sure you have a good sense of what has happened so far in the reading before continuing. This strategy of breaking a reading up can be particularly useful when reading about historical time periods or in reading fiction where you need to keep track of times, dates, and events.

Practice Activity: Breaking a Reading into Manageable Chunks

Break Reading 2 into manageable chunks by following these steps.

1. Notice there are two sections that roughly divide the reading into half.

2. Draw a line above the subhead "Jeffersonian Vistas."

3. For more practice, divide this first section in half too. Draw another line between Paragraphs 5 and 6.

4. Then in the second half of the reading, draw another line between Paragraphs 15 and 16.

5. Now, you have manageable chunks that you can read carefully. As you read later, use the time between chunks to make sure you understand.

During Reading Strategy: Asking Questions as You Read

A helpful strategy used by good readers is asking themselves questions as they read. In many ways, it doesn't matter what questions you ask yourself, as long as you do ask questions because it helps you focus on the topic. Questions can help you check your level of understanding, particularly when you are reading about a topic that is new or unfamiliar to you or when the text is very dense.

You should always ask questions about the most important details. Since you have broken the reading up, your questions may be related to the number of pieces or chunks, like:

1. Do I need more chunks? Fewer?

2. What events or vocabulary should I look up after I read each section?

Practice Activity: Asking Questions as You Read

Using the suggested manageable chunks from the activity on page 200, read each section of the reading you created, and then answer these questions.

Section 1

1. What is the most important thing that happens in this section?

2. What people or events are important to remember from this section?

Section 2

1. What is the most important thing that happens in this section?

2. What people or events are important to remember from this section?

Section 3

1. What is the most important thing that happens in this section?

   _____

2. What people or events are important to remember from this section?

   _____

Section 4

1. What is the most important thing that happens in this section?

   _____

2. What people or events are important to remember from this section?

   _____

Now that you have read the reading in its entirety, what do you think are the most important pieces of information and the most important events and people?

_____

_____

_____

_____

_____

_____

_____

_____

Vocabulary Power

There are a number of terms and phrases in this reading that you may encounter in other academic settings. Add at least five vocabulary items to your vocabulary notebook or log.

Match the words in bold from the reading on the left with a definition on the right.

1. _____ At least on the face of it, this triumphal tone seems wholly **justified**.

2. _____ At less than 4 cents an acre, the Purchase became the most **lucrative** real estate transaction in American history, easily besting the purchase of Manhattan for $24.

3. _____ Although the term "manifest destiny" had not yet been **coined**, the Purchase made the idea another one of those self evident truths.

4. _____ On the American side, there are Thomas Jefferson and James Madison, working their **collaborative** magic.

5. _____ There were several reasons for this **omission**, and modesty was not one of them

6. _____ An appropriate starting point is March 6, 1801, as Jefferson **ascended** to the presidency after one of the most controversial elections in American history.

7. _____ . . . a reduction of the national debt, made possible by a **slashing** of all federal budgets. . . .

8. _____ . . . he shared with most Virginians including George Washington, the **keen** sense that Europe was the past and the American west was the future.

a. profitable

b. right or fair

c. rose or advanced

d. cut sharply

e. created

f. intelligent

g. teamed, with others

h. something left out or removed

Reading

Now, read the passage. Answer the questions on pages 201–2 as you read each chunk.

The Purchase

(1) The story of the Louisiana Purchase has many twists and turns, and the biggest challenge in retelling it is to avoid getting caught in the diplomatic aspects of years before 1803.

(2) It is widely acknowledged that the Louisiana Purchase, in the end, was a triumph on a par with the winning of independence and the adoption of the Constitution. Frederick Jackson Turner, the founding father of western history, also described the Purchase as the formative event in the national narrative: "Having taken the decisive stride across the Mississippi, the United States enlarged the horizon of her views, and marched steadily forward to the possession of the Pacific Ocean. From this event dates the rise of the United States into a position of world power."

(3) At least on the face of it, this triumphal tone seems wholly justified. For $15 million—the rough equivalent of $260 million today—the United States doubled its size, adding what is now the American Midwest to the national domain, all the land from the Mississippi to the Rocky Mountains and the Canadian border to the Gulf of Mexico. At less than 4 cents an acre, the Purchase became the most lucrative real estate transaction in American history, easily besting the purchase of Manhattan for $24. Without quite knowing it, the United States had acquired the most fertile tract of land of its size on the

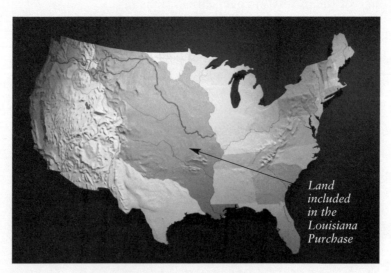

Land included in the Louisiana Purchase

planet, making it self-sufficient in food in the nineteenth century and the agrarian superpower in the twentieth.

(4) There was more. Politically, the Louisiana Purchase was the most consequential executive decision in American history, rivaled only by Harry Truman's decision to drop the atomic bomb in 1945. It is interesting to note that the man who made the decision, Thomas Jefferson, was on record as believing that any projection of executive power was an act suitable only to a monarchy. Strategically, the Purchase opened a new chapter in American national security by removing, in one fell swoop, all British and French imperial ambitions in North America.

(5) Spain remained the only European power blocking American expansion to the Pacific, and Spain was not so much threatening power as a convenient presence, in effect awaiting an American takeover at the appropriate time. Although the term "manifest destiny"* had not yet been coined, the Purchase made the idea another one of those self evident truths. A colossal and fully continental American empire was now almost inevitable. If the Mississippi ends at New Orleans and the Gulf of Mexico, the story of the Purchase (at least its triumphal version) ends at the Pacific.

manifest destiny:
an event that hasn't happened yet, but is inevitable or certain; a term often used in connection with westward expansion in the United States in the 1800s

(6) As befitting an epic story, this one has an all-star international cast. On the American side, there are Thomas Jefferson and James Madison, working their collaborative magic. The Paris delegation is headed by James Monroe, perhaps the most loyal Jefferson protégé of all, and Robert Livingston, a member of New York's elite who actually sealed the deal. The French side has Napoleon Bonaparte, already the most famous and feared man in the world.

(7) Jefferson's genius was to seize that time, and to recognize that acquiring an empire required an imperial president. Given the peaceful way the Purchase occurred, it might be more accurate to think of it as the perfect calm, and of Jefferson's greatest diplomatic talent as the patience to stand still while history formed around him.

(8) Given the triumphal tone of most histories of the Purchase, and the somewhat silly scramble to assign credit for the triumph, it is curious that Jefferson himself made a point of not listing it on his tombstone as one of his proudest achievements. Nor did he list his presidency, in which the Purchase was unquestionable his singular accomplishment. There were several reasons for this omission, and modesty was not one of them.

(9) There is a tragic as well as triumphal version of the story. As the triumphal version moved gloriously and inexorably toward the Pacific, the tragic moved ominously toward the Civil War, whose immediate cause was the debate over slavery in the territory Jefferson had done so much to acquire. Indeed, the tragedy was double-barreled, since the Louisiana Purchase also proved to be the death knell for any Native American presence east of the Mississippi. And since the failure to end slavery and the failure to preserve and protect the indigenous peoples of North America were the two great stains on the legacy of the founding generation, the fact that the Purchase locked these failures into place was not an achievement Jefferson wished to advertise.

(10) An appropriate starting point is March 6, 1801, as Jefferson ascended to the presidency after one of the most controversial elections in American history. In his inaugural address, destined to become one of the best, he outlined the principles that would guide him, which were essentially the same principles that shaped the agenda of the Republican party over the past decade: "A wise and frugal government which . . . shall not take from the mouth of labour the bread it earned"; a reduction of the national debt, made possible by a slashing of all federal budgets and a transfer of all domestic policies to the states; an innocuous and almost invisible executive branch, rendered even more inconspicuous by Jefferson's decision to file all presidential correspondence with the relevant cabinet officers in order to eliminate even a presidential paper trail. These were "the ancient Whig* principles," the values of "pure republicanism" that the Federalists had betrayed. These were the cherished principles Jefferson proclaimed. With the Louisiana Purchase, he was about to violate every of them.

Whig: a political party in the United States in the 1830s, '40s, and '50s

Jeffersonian Vistas

(11) Although Jefferson never traveled further west than the Natural Bridge in Shenandoah Valley, he shared with most Virginians including George Washington, the keen sense that Europe was the past and the American west was the future. Both men misguidedly believed that the Potomac was a strategically placed water route over the Alleghenies into the interior of the country, linking the Ohio and then flowing into the Mississippi Valley. This was not true, but this inconvenient fact did little to deflect the westward flow of Jefferson's thinking, which, as it turned out, was even more grandiose than Washington's.

(12) A few months after he took office, Jefferson shared his vision with James Monroe, then serving as governor of Virginia: "It is impossible not to look forward to distant times," Jefferson observed, "when our rapid multiplication will . . . cover the whole northern, if not southern continent with a people speaking the same language, governed in similar forms, and by similar laws; nor can we contemplate with satisfaction either blot or mixture on that surface."

(13) This Jeffersonian vision depended upon two crucial assumptions. At the time of his election, the census of 1800 revealed a total population of slightly more than five million, with about 500,000 residing west of the Alleghenies. Jefferson assumed that the western population would steadily swell and move the frontier gradually but inexorably forward to the Mississippi and beyond. Unlike Washington, he did not believe that this wave of settlers could or should be managed by the federal government. It was like a force of nature that must be allowed its own momentum. The lands to the west did not need to be conquered by armies, but rather occupied by settlers. In that sense, it was demography that made American destiny so manifest. The only role for government was to stay out of the way and allow the wave to roll westward.

(14) The second assumption was that the only European power with a substantial presence on the North American continent would be Spain. A map of the Spanish Empire in the Western Hemisphere in 1800 made Spain's colonial empire appear gigantic, including Florida, the Gulf Coast, and all the land west of the Mississippi to the Pacific, not to mention Mexico and much of South America. But the map was deceptive in its grandeur because Spain was a hollowed-out imperial power, in decline since the defeat of the Spanish Armada in 1588.

(15) By 1800 the treasury in Madrid was empty, the Spanish army and navy were harmless pretenders, and the once proud diplomatic corps was adept only at posturing. His only fear was that the Spanish Empire was so weak that it would abandon its American colonies "before our population can be sufficiently advanced to gain it from them piece by piece."

(16) Only three weeks after the inauguration, Jefferson received a message from Secretary of State Madison. The American ambassador to Great Britain, Rufus King, reported reliable rumors circulating in London that Spain had signed a secret treaty, ceding fully half of her North American colonies to France. If true, this transformed the entire strategic chemistry in North America by replacing the most feeble European nation with what had become under Napoleon the most potent military power on earth. For several months Jefferson monitored reports from Europe, most of which tended to confirm that Napoleon fully intended to reestablish the French Empire in America. Jefferson could only hope they were untrue.

(17) By the spring of 1803, all such hoping had become a sentimental extravagance, since the secret treaty ceding Louisiana to France had become the worst-kept secret in Europe. Pushing the quite capable Madison aside, Jefferson chose to become his own secretary of state. For the simple truth was that the French occupation of Louisiana would be unmitigated calamity for the United States, constituting the greatest threat to American destiny since the Revolutionary War: "It completely reverses all the political relations of the United States and will form a new epoch in our political course . . . There is on the globe one single spot, the possessor of which is our natural and habitual enemy. It is New Orleans." Spanish control of New Orleans was not threatening, since— Spain being Spain—the outcome of a conflict was certain. But French possession was another matter altogether. "From that moment," wrote Jefferson, "we must marry ourselves to the British fleet and nation."

(18) This was an extraordinary statement coming from Jefferson, whose entire career as minister to France, secretary of state, and leader of the Republican opposition to the Jay Treaty had consistently favored France over Great Britain as America's most reliable European ally. But he was prepared to reverse himself once France became a threatening presence on the North American continent and a formidable challenge to America's demographic destiny.

(19) Jefferson then made an extremely shrewd observation. On the face of it, a war with France was a suicidal venture, given the enormous discrepancy in military and economic resources. But all such assessments were irrelevant and misleading, "for however greater the force is than ours, compared in the abstract, it is nothing compared to ours, when to be exerted on our own soil." If Napoleon attempted to establish a French Empire in America by force of arms, he would encounter the same dilemma as the British in the War for Independence, marching among a hostile population over a space even more immense. Livingston was instructed to apprise the French that if they attempted to occupy the Louisiana Territory, they would suffer the same fate as the British, for space and numbers were both on the American side.

(20) Any European nation that threatened Napoleon in this fashion usually found itself defeated and occupied. But space—both the Atlantic Ocean and the sheer vastness of the American interior—was a priceless strategic asset that no European nation could match. Jefferson practiced what has come to be called "back-channel diplomacy" by soliciting the assistance of a prominent French aristocrat, Pierre Samuel Du Pont de Nemours, to carry Livingston's instructions back to Paris and then to quietly disseminate within the corridors of power the same threatening message conveyed to Livingston. "If France proceeds to possess New Orleans," Jefferson told Du Pont, "we must marry ourselves to the British fleet and nation." Though this had the clear ring of an ultimatum, Jefferson wanted Du Pont—and eventually Napoleon—to know that he regarded war with France as a last resort. "You know how much I value peace," he explained, "and how unwillingly I should see an event take place that would render war a necessary resource."

(21) Jefferson was utterly sincere on this score, since war, even a successful war, would completely destroy his domestic agenda of debt reduction and minimalist government. And an alliance with Great Britain would contradict every foreign policy principle he had ever championed. Indeed, it is entirely possible that Jefferson's war threat was actually a bluff. The preferred alternative for both sides, Jefferson informed Du Pont and Livingston, was a diplomatic resolution of the crisis. The United States was prepared to offer $6 million for the purchase of New Orleans and West Florida (the Gulf Coast from modern-day Pensacola to New Orleans). If Napoleon accepted this offer, the United States was, albeit reluctantly, prepared to accept French possession of the entire Louisiana Territory west of the Mississippi.

(22) This was a huge concession. It is likely, though not certain, that Jefferson regarded any French presence in Louisiana as temporary. Once the advancing wave of American population reached the Mississippi, or, as Jefferson put it, "once we have planted such a population on the Mississippi as will be able to do their business," the French position would become untenable because the Americans could mobilize an overwhelming force "without necessary of marching men from the shores of the Atlantic 1500 or 2000 miles hither." Again, space, and more specifically space that was "peopled," was a unique and in calculable strategic advantage that Jefferson was prepared to exploit. But such scenarios all lay in the future. For now, the immediate crisis required a peaceful resolution.

After Reading Strategy: Improving Retention and Recall

An important academic skill involves being able to retain information about what you have read and to recall it when needed. This may mean that your instructor literally asks you in class the next day to explain what you read, but it also may come up in written assignments or on exams later in the course.

When you read your course assignments or do other types of readings on an important topic, take a minute or two when you are done to make some notes in the book (if it's not a library book) or in your notebook that will help you remember the important parts of the reading. Sometimes, what you write might be a reference to something else. For example, it might be that some parts of "The Farewell" (about George Washington) reminds you of something that happened with another leader in another time period or in another country. In that case, it may simply be enough to write "similar to Bolivar in Venezuela."

It's not so important WHAT you write, as long as it is something that will help you retain the basic information and be able to recall it when needed.

Practice Activity: Improving Retention and Recall

Answer these question, and then discuss them with a partner.

1. Review the two readings in Unit 4. What do you remember about each of these readings?

   _____

   _____

2. Go back to the two readings in Unit 5. What do you remember about each of these readings?

   _____

   _____

3. Do you think you remembered enough? What notes would you add to the book to help you retain information from those readings now?

   _____

   _____

Practice Activity: Reading for the Big Picture

Put a check mark (✓) next to the statements that best reflects the main ideas.

1. _____ The Louisiana Purchase was one of Jefferson's most executive decisions.

2. _____ The Louisiana Purchase was a far better deal than the purchase of Manhattan.

3. _____ The atomic bomb as an equally important event.

4. _____ The Louisiana Purchase was both a tragedy and a triumph.

5. _____ Jefferson's vision depended on the population of the States and the power of Spain.

6. _____ Jefferson was not worried about Mississippi or the West.

Paraphrasing to Simplify

Write a paraphrase that expresses the main points of the original without re-using too many words or phrases from the original.

1. . . . this inconvenient fact did little to deflect the westward flow of Jefferson's thinking, which, as it turned out, was even more grandiose than Washington's.

   _____

   _____

2. Jefferson assumed that the western population would steadily swell and move the frontier gradually but inexorably forward to the Mississippi and beyond.

   _____

   _____

3. If Napoleon attempted to establish a French Empire in America by force of arms, he would encounter the same dilemma as the British in the War for Independence, marching among a hostile population over a space even more immense.

   _____

   _____

Writing Strategy: Considering Your Audience

It is important to remember that you are writing for someone else. Your audience can change. Sometimes it may be your instructor, other times it may be a group of people studying the same topic as you, and yet other times it may be a general group of people that don't know you or your topic. Considering who your audience is will help you decide what content to include, the best way to organize, and the vocabulary you should use.

You should ask yourself questions before you begin writing.

- Who is in my audience?
- What do my audience members need?
- Do I think they have any prior knowledge about this topic?
- What would be the most important things for them to know?
- What would be the most interesting things for them to read?
- How detailed do I need to be?

Practice Activity: Considering Your Audience

Read these assignments and the audiences given. Then talk with a partner about answers to the questions from the box on page 212.

1. You need to write a paper for your history classmates about the differences between Washington and Jefferson.

   _____

   _____

   _____

2. Describe to a group of economics students why the Louisiana Purchase was a landmark decision for Jefferson.

   _____

   _____

   _____

3. Write an essay for your history professor about Jefferson's role in the Louisiana Purchase.

   _____

   _____

   _____

4. Write a letter to a relative about what you've learned about Thomas Jefferson.

   _____

   _____

   _____

5. Explain to your roommate who Jefferson's close colleagues were.

   _____

   _____

   _____

Your Active Vocabulary in the Real World

Vocabulary is important. Some words are useful for your speaking or for your writing, but other words are useful for your reading or your listening. For each word, decide how you think you will probably need this word for your English. Put a check mark (✓) under the ways you think you are likely to need the word. It is possible to have a check mark in more than one column.

	YOUR VOCABULARY	I need to be able to use this word in WRITING.	I need to be able to use this word in SPEAKING.	I need to understand this word in READING.	I need to understand this word in LISTENING.
1.	acquire				
2.	decisive				
3.	epic				
4.	expansion				
5.	lucrative				
6.	power				
7.	presidency				
8.	real estate				
9.	transaction				
10.	triumph				

Rapid Vocabulary Review

From the three answers on the right, circle the one that best explains, is an example of, or combines with vocabulary word on the left as it is used in this unit.

Vocabulary	Answers		
Synonyms			
1. contemplate	think about	worry about	talk about
2. stable	unconvincing	unchanging	uninteresting
3. abandon	leave	save	receive
4. feeble	big	secret	weak
5. resolution	concern	issue	solution
6. perennial	contrast	occasional	rare
7. landmark	average	notable	truth
8. subsequent	first	next	recent
9. indispensable	necessary	serious	transparent
10. concession	admission	among	threat
11. temporary	limited time	permanent	threat
12. exploit	to attack	to sell fast	to use unfairly
Combinations and Associations			
13. twists and _____	tales	talks	turns
14. on a par _____	at	in	with
15. executive _____	decision	farm	space
16. seal the _____	deal	papers	presidency
17. make a _____	challenge	favor	point
18. a debate _____ a topic	about	to	up
19. double-_____	barreled	failed	moved
20. _____ office	make	give	take

⇔⇔ Synthesizing: Writing Projects

In-Class Writing Assignments	Outside Assignments
Thinking about the Future	Good or Bad?
Because the country was so new when Washington and Jefferson were presidents, what obligations did they have to consider how their decisions would affect the future? Compare and contrast their experiences with a more current U.S. president or world leader. **Suggested Length:** 300 words **Preparation:** none	Was Washington's decision to leave the presidency ultimately good for the new nation? What about Thomas Jefferson's decision to make the Louisiana Purchase? Work with a group to do some research on the history of America since 1796, and decide if these were good decisions. Create a group paper on your group's ideas about the impact of their decisions on the country as it is now. **Suggested Length:** 800 words **Preparation:** Light research in a library or online
What Were They Thinking?	When You're the First
Think about what you've read in this unit, and then write an essay that answers this question: Which actions of George Washington and Thomas Jefferson demonstrate how they viewed their role as President of the United States? Support your answer with examples from the readings. **Suggested Length:** 500 words **Preparation:** none	Select one of these decisions made by another U.S. president, and decide if these decisions were good or bad for the country or world. Do research. • Abraham Lincoln ends slavery (1863) • Franklin Roosevelt declares war on Germany and Japan (1941) • Lyndon Johnson deepens involvement in Vietnam (1965) • George W. Bush invades Iraq (2003) **Suggested Length:** 1,000 words **Preparation:** Light research in a library or online

Vocabulary Log

To increase your vocabulary knowledge, write a definition or translation for each vocabulary item. Then write an original phrase, sentence, or note that will help you remember the vocabulary item.

Vocabulary Item	Definition or Translation	Your Original Phrase, Sentence, or Note
1. colossal	huge	a colossal mistake
2. omnipotence		
3. surveyed		
4. rally		
5. indispensable		
6. contemporary (n.)		
7. struck home (v.)		
8. precedent		
9. paper trail		
10. legend		
11. inevitable		
12. genius		
13. principles		
14. eliminate		

Vocabulary Item	Definition or Translation	Your Original Phrase, Sentence, or Note
15. proclaim (v.)		
16. deflect		
17. assumptions		
18. inexorably		
19. demography		
20. manifest		
21. destiny		
22. adept		
23. calamity		
24. formidable		
25. reliable		